IEG WORLD BANK | IFC | MIGA
INDEPENDENT EVALUATION GROUP

Egypt: Positive Results from Knowledge Sharing and Modest Lending

An IEG Country Assistance Evaluation 1999–2007

2009
The World Bank
Washington, D.C.

http://www.worldbank.org/ieg

1818 H Street NW
Washington DC 20433
Telephone: 202-473-1000
Internet: www.worldbank.org
E-mail: feedback@worldbank.org

1 2 3 4 12 11 10 09

Cover: Top: Pyramids of Egypt. © Jose Fuste Raga/Corbis. Bottom: The Nile at Cairo. © Christophe Boisvieux/Corbis.

ISBN-13: 978-0-8213-7958-5
e-ISBN-13: 978-0-8213-7959-2
DOI: 10.1596/978-0-8213-7958-5

Library of Congress Cataloging-in-Publication Data have been applied for.

World Bank InfoShop
E-mail: pic@worldbank.org
Telephone: 202-458-5454
Facsimile: 202-522-1500

Printed on Recycled Paper

Independent Evaluation Group
Knowledge Programs and Evaluation Capacity Development (IEGKE)
E-mail: ieg@worldbank.org
Telephone: 202-458-4497
Facsimile: 202-522-3125

Contents

Abbreviations

AAA	Analytical and advisory assistance
AfDB	African Development Bank
CAE	Country Assistance Evaluation
CAS	Country Assistance Strategy
DPL	Development policy loan
EEAA	Egyptian Environmental Affairs Agency
EPAP	Egypt Pollution Abatement Project
EU	European Union
FDI	Foreign direct investment
FSAP	Financial Sector Assessment Program
GDP	Gross domestic product
GNI	Gross national income
IBRD	International Bank for Reconstruction and Development
ICA	Investment climate assessment
IDA	International Development Association
IEG	Independent Evaluation Group
IFC	International Finance Corporation
IMF	International Monetary Fund
IPP	Independent power producer
kWh	Kilowatt hours
MW	Megawatts
NCW	National Council of Women
PCR/TAS	Project completion report/technical advisory services (IFC)
PEP-MENA	Private Enterprise Partnership for the Middle East and North Africa
PER	Public Expenditure Review
PFM	Public financial management
PPP	Public-private partnerships
PSG	Public sector governance
SFD	Social Fund for Development
SME	Small and medium-size enterprise
TA	Technical assistance
TSA	Treasury Single Account
UNDP	United Nations Development Programme
USAID	United States Agency for International Development

Irrigation improvement project, financed by the World Bank. Photo courtesy of the Irrigation Improvement Sector.

Acknowledgments

This Country Assistance Evaluation was written by Ismail Arslan, with contributions by consultants Ataman Aksoy, David Berk, Laurie Effron, James Fox, Joseph Goldberg, Omar Lyasse, and Victor Orozco. The peer reviewers were Susanne Muller (Harvard University), John Nash (Latin American and the Caribbean Region Sustainable Development Department, World Bank), Marilou Uy (Africa Region Finance and Private Sector Development Department, World Bank), and Steven Webb (Independent Evaluation Group–Country Evaluation and Regional Relations [IEGCR]). A review of International Finance Corporation operations in the Arab Republic of Egypt during this period was prepared by Cherian Samuel and Izlem Yenice (IEG–International Finance Corporation) and is included in appendix B. William Hurlbut provided editorial assistance. Production and logistical support was provided by Agnes Santos. Heather Dittbrenner copy edited the study for publication.

Director-General, Evaluation: *Vinod Thomas*
Director, Independent Evaluation Group–World Bank: *Cheryl W. Gray*
Senior Manager, Country Evaluation and Regional Relations Unit: *Ali M. Khadr**
Task Manager: *Ismail Arslan*

* Ali M. Khadr, Senior Manager, IEGCR, recused himself from management oversight of this evaluation, owing to his past position as Sector Manager in the Middle East and North Africa Region during the period 1998–2000.

Over the last several years, Egypt has implemented a series of important reforms that have led to solid performance. The country has been ranked in the top 10 reformers under Doing Business for three consecutive years. Photo courtesy of Victor Orozco, World Bank Group.

Foreword

This Country Assistance Evaluation reviews World Bank support to the Arab Republic of Egypt from fiscal 1999 through 2007. Egypt's economic performance over the period improved substantially. This was particularly true after 2004, following improvements in economic management, an increase in the pace of structural reforms, and correction of the exchange rate. Gross domestic product growth averaged about 5 percent over the period, rising to almost 7 percent in 2006 and 2007. Human development indicators improved significantly. However, progress in poverty reduction has been disappointing, with a deterioration in the poverty headcount, particularly in Upper Egypt.

Overall, the Bank's financial assistance to Egypt has been modest. From fiscal 1999 to 2007, the Bank committed $2.1 billion for 18 investment projects and one policy-based loan. Bank analytical work has helped in the design of recent economic reforms and in monitoring poverty. The International Finance Corporation (IFC) has also been active, with loans and investments totaling $842 million across a diversified portfolio, and collaboration between the International Bank for Reconstruction and Development (IBRD) and IFC in Egypt has been adequate.

Bank strategy focused on promoting higher, more sustainable growth through structural reforms. The Bank's support for financial sector reform was particularly effective and covered among other things the restructuring and privatization of state-owned banks. Import tariffs were simplified and lowered, personal income and corporate tax rates were reduced and the tax base broadened, and tax administration reform progressed. Nevertheless, although budget deficits have declined, they remain high, and inflationary pressure from strong domestic demand and rising world food prices persists, posing risks to macroeconomic stability.

The Bank also focused on development of water resources, infrastructure, and environment. For three decades, the Bank has been Egypt's principal development partner in irrigation and water management; the largely renewed irrigation system has contributed to recent increases in agriculture productivity and exports. Bank efforts to support the development of rural finance have been less successful. The Bank was absent from infrastructure during this period until 2004, when it financed large air transportation and energy projects. In the environmental sector, the Bank had two small loans and carried out several studies. Limited progress was made in improving water and air pollution.

The results of Bank support for human development and poverty reduction assistance were mixed. The support focused on access and quality of basic services, as well as on managing population growth. Gender disparities in education and health were reduced substantially during the review period. The Bank's inputs contributed significantly to the present strength of the National Council of Women. Progress in reducing poverty and inequality, however, was elusive. The poverty headcount rose from 16.7 percent in 2000 to 19.6 percent in 2005, although it may have fallen with the strong economic growth in the past two years. A crucial issue is the incidence of poverty in rural Upper Egypt, where the poverty headcount is twice the national average.

Future Bank strategy needs to reflect Egypt's middle-income status by including a flexible lending program and an emphasis on knowledge services, including reimbursable technical assistance. The Bank can further strengthen the partnership by focusing on (i) the persistent issue of poverty and inequality; (ii) analytic work on macroeconomic analysis and income disparities and its improved dissemination; (iii) further financial sector reforms and promoting continued reforms in systems that indirectly combat corruption; and (iv) sectoral strategies and policy and institutional reforms in infrastructure and energy.

Vinod Thomas
Director-General, Evaluation

Preface

This Country Assistance Evaluation (CAE) provides an independent assessment of World Bank assistance to the Arab Republic of Egypt during the period fiscal 1999–2007. The CAE examines whether (i) the objectives of Bank assistance were relevant (that is, whether they were the "right" ones in light of the country's needs and priorities as well as the Bank's comparative advantage), (ii) the Bank's assistance program was effectively designed and consistent with its objectives, and (iii) the Bank's program achieved its targets. Examining these questions allows the CAE to draw lessons and recommendations for future Bank assistance. Appendix D describes the methodological approach for the evaluation.

The evaluation is based on a review of World Bank documents and on interviews with senior government officials, representatives of the private sector and civil society, nongovernmental organizations, members of the donor community, and Bank and International Monetary Fund staff in Washington and in Egypt. A list of those interviewed is in appendix C. An Independent Evaluation Group mission visited Egypt in July and October 2007.

The Management Action Record is presented after the Executive Summary. Comments from the Bank's regional management have been incorporated in the report. The report was also sent to the Egyptian authorities; their comments are reflected in the report and appear in appendix E.

Worker on construction site of water project, one of many supported by the Bank. Photo by Ray Witlin, courtesy of the World Bank Photo Library.

Egypt: Summary of Bank Program Outcome Ratings

Bank strategic goals[a]	Achievement of associated Country Assistance Strategy outcomes or results	Bank program outcome ratings[b]
First pillar: Promoting higher, more sustainable growth through structural reforms	**Relative macroeconomic stability and higher growth were notable achievements, although progress was slow in reducing fiscal deficits and public debt. Trade, regulatory, and financial sector reforms progressed well.**	**Moderately satisfactory**
Maintain macroeconomic stability and improve public sector governance	There were policy reversals and deterioration of fiscal balances and debt/gross national product ratios as well as economic slowdown between 2000 and 2003. Fiscal and monetary policy improved after 2004. Government debt management strengthened. Progress was made in improving public procurement and transparency of the budget. Pension reform is under way.	Moderately satisfactory
Trade policy and administration reform	The trade regime was very restrictive until major reforms started in 2005. The trade and foreign exchange regimes were significantly reformed with large increases in trade to gross domestic product ratios. Customs administration and regulations were streamlined. Foreign direct investment inflows and exports increased significantly.	Moderately satisfactory
Private sector development and regulatory environment	There were many barriers to entry and to operations of private enterprises, and the privatization program was inactive in the 1999–2004 period. However, the business environment and regulations improved. Significant improvements were made in licensing, taxation, and registration. The privatization program has been revived.	Satisfactory
Financial sector reform	Progress was made on a new banking law and other regulatory reforms and on strengthening of supervision of banks and nonbank financial institutions starting in 2004. One large public bank was privatized. The Central Bank's capacity was enhanced. Banking system finances were much stronger at the end of the review period.	Satisfactory
Second pillar: Water resources management, infrastructure, and environment	**Bank projects supported major expansion and upgrading of irrigation systems, airports, and power generation. The telecommunications sector was liberalized. There was limited progress in environmental protection.**	**Satisfactory**
Improve water resources management, agriculture, and rural development	Good performance was posted on irrigation, drainage, and pumping infrastructure investments. Water users' associations became operational, leading to effective involvement of farmers in water resources management. Agricultural sector performance improved. No progress was made in reducing regional income differences (Lower versus Upper Egypt).	Satisfactory

Bank strategic goals[a]	Achievement of associated Country Assistance Strategy outcomes or results	Bank program outcome ratings[b]
Enhance civil aviation, telecommunications, and energy infrastructure	Airports underwent substantial expansion and upgrading. The telecommunications sector was liberalized and the National Telecommunications Regulatory Agency established. Installed power generation capacity increased.	Satisfactory
Strengthen environmental management	Monitoring and enforcement improved at the national and local levels. Limited improvements occurred in air, water, and solid waste pollution indicators. The Environment Affairs Agency was given greater authority.	Moderately satisfactory
Third pillar: Human development and poverty reduction	**Although many human development indicators improved, poverty headcount increased to 19.6 percent in 2004–05 from 16.7 percent in 2000, after declining in the late 1990s. Poverty remains concentrated in rural areas and in Upper Egypt.**	**Moderately satisfactory**
Reduce gender disparities	Gender issues were mainstreamed to a considerable extent, and disparities fell substantially in education and health. Female unemployment declined. The capacity of the National Council of Women increased.	Satisfactory
Improve access and quality of education services	The primary education gross enrollment rate remained at 101 percent, and the secondary ratio increased from 75 to 86 percent. There were modest improvements in education quality.	Satisfactory
Improve health status of population	Health indicators improved. Infant mortality rate declined from 44 to 33 per 1,000 births. Births attended by skilled staff rose sharply from 46 to 74 percent. Bank contribution has been limited, however.	Moderately satisfactory
Strengthen social safety nets and subsidy program	The institutional structure for the food subsidy program was improved, but existing in-kind subsidy programs continue to be costly and benefit the rich more than the poor. Social Development Fund programs had good outcomes.	Moderately unsatisfactory
Overall	**The Bank's program facilitated important policy and structural changes in the Egyptian economy, mostly from 2004 onward, which have supported high economic growth rates in recent years. Business climate improvements have amplified the benefits of trade, private sector development, and financial sector reforms. Social indicators have also improved. Despite these positive developments, progress on reducing poverty and inequality has been disappointing.**	**Moderately satisfactory**

a. The goals of Bank assistance may be distinct from those of the client country's own development objectives, although the two are usually consistent.
b. The Bank program outcome subratings and overall rating assess the extent to which the Bank program achieved the results targeted in the relevant strategy document(s) and/or the documents for individual operations. They do not attempt to assess the extent to which the client country was satisfied with the Bank's program, nor do they try to measure the extent (in an absolute sense) to which the program contributed to the country's development. Equally, they are not synonymous with Bank performance.

Executive Summary

Between fiscal 1999 and 2007, the period under review in this Country Assistance Evaluation (CAE), the Arab Republic of Egypt's economic performance improved substantially. This was particularly true after 2004, following improvements in economic management, structural reforms, and correction of the exchange rate. The gross domestic product (GDP) growth rate averaged about 5 percent per year over this period, rising to almost 7 percent in 2006 and 2007. This translates into a per capita income growth of almost 3 percent per year, a strong performance.

The Bank's financial assistance to Egypt has been modest (providing only about 4 percent of total official development assistance) compared with that of other donors, particularly the U.S. Agency for International Development (USAID). From fiscal 1999 to 2007, International Development Association (IDA)/International Bank for Reconstruction and Development (IBRD) commitments amounted to $2.1 billion for 18 investment credits and one policy-based loan. The country graduated from IDA in June 1999. The Bank's assistance program largely met its objectives and contributed significantly to policy and institutional changes, especially in the financial sector, privatization, pension system, and private sector development. For three decades the Bank has been Egypt's principal development partner in irrigation and water management, and the largely renewed irrigation system has contributed to recent increases in agriculture productivity and exports. Bank efforts in rural finance have been less successful. The Bank has also contributed to improvements in Egypt's human development indicators, although large income disparities persist between Lower and Upper Egypt.

Future Bank strategy should reflect Egypt's middle-income status by including a flexible lending program and an emphasis on knowledge services, including reimbursable technical assistance. The Bank can further strengthen the recent successful partnership by (i) identifying direct and indirect interventions that could help reduce income disparities through improving the targeting of social safety nets; (ii) focusing analytic work on macroeconomic analysis and income disparities and improving its dissemination; (iii) pursuing further financial sector reforms and promoting reforms that indirectly combat corruption (public financial management, simplification of taxation and business procedures, and an information act); and (iv) emphasizing sectoral strategies and policy and institutional reforms in infrastructure and energy.

Background

Egypt is a country of more than 74 million people and a per capita income of $1,580 (as of 2006), occupying a crucial position in the geopolitics of the Middle East. Less than 5 percent of Egypt's total land area is cultivated, the remainder being uninhabitable desert. Thus, more than 97 percent of the population lives in the narrow strip of the highly fertile Nile valley and its delta. There are major differences in poverty and inequality across regions in Egypt, with the highest poverty in Upper Egypt (south), both rural and urban, and the lowest in metropolitan areas and Lower Egypt (north). Social equity and political stability have been continuing concerns, reflected in the allocation of significant public resources to social spending.

Prior to the period under review, Egypt had begun a program of stabilization and structural reform, supported by donors. The combination of fiscal discipline, exchange rate and modest trade reforms, some price liberalization, and selected privatizations yielded results: inflation came down from over 20 percent in 1991 to below 10 percent in 1995, while GDP growth rose from the stagnation of the early 1990s to 4.7 percent in 1995. In addition, partly as a result of the 1991 Paris Club agreement on external debt restructuring, the debt was reduced from very high levels (Egypt was one of the most heavily indebted countries in the world in the late 1980s) to a modest 60 percent of GDP by 1995.

In 1996, the government further deepened earlier reforms. Although fiscal deficits began to increase again, private investment grew to almost 13 percent of GDP in 1998 compared to less than 10 percent in the early 1990s; growth was 5.3 percent per annum between 1995 and 2000; and inflation continued to decline to less than 4 percent by 1998. Thus, at the beginning of the period under review, Egypt had been undergoing a series of economic reforms that had yielded positive results.

Bank Assistance

During the CAE period, Bank assistance to Egypt was guided by three Country Assistance Strategies (CASs) in 1997, 2001, and 2005. Their dominant and consistent themes were (i) promotion of higher, more sustainable economic growth through structural reforms; (ii) development of water resources, infrastructure, and the environment; and (iii) development of human resources and poverty reduction. The focus of the CASs was relevant and consistent with the key development objectives of the government, but both the 1997 and 2001 CASs were overly optimistic about the amounts and focus of Bank lending that could be put in place and about the government's willingness to use policy-based lending. Although governance was not an explicit objective of the Bank's strategy and program, the Bank was able to find an entry point through the investment climate assessments to provide input into anticorruption efforts.

From fiscal 1999 to 2007, IDA/IBRD approved $2.1 billion for 18 investment credits and one policy-based (adjustment) loan. This was modest relative to official aid flows, representing only about 4 percent of total aid (between fiscal 1999 and 2005, the latest year for which data are available on official aid). For almost four years following Egypt's graduation from IDA in 1999, the government was reluctant to borrow significant amounts on IBRD terms, and lending declined to about $30 million per year.

During this period, the Bank focused on economic and sector work and on cleaning up the problem projects in the portfolio. The late addition of a large airports development project in fiscal 2004, not foreseen in the CAS, changed the dynamic, and combined with a new reform-oriented government, the Bank's assistance began to ramp up. The Bank provided key analytic work in poverty, investment climate, financial sector, energy, and environment, partly through a new instrument—reimbursable technical assistance—and established fruitful policy dialogue in a number of key ministries. The Bank made a large development policy loan in support of wide-ranging financial sector reforms. The quality of the Bank's portfolio improved dramatically, with a reduction in the portfolio at risk and an improvement in disbursement rates. Over the CAE period, the International Finance Corporation (IFC) was active, with loans and investments totaling $842 million across a diversified portfolio and delivery of advisory services totaling $12 million.

Findings of the Evaluation

Under the first pillar—*promotion of higher, more sustainable growth through structural reforms*—outcomes of the CAS objectives were uneven, slower to materialize in the first part of the period, but good in the latter period. Between 1999 and 2003, economic growth slowed, averaging only around 3.2 percent per annum, accompanied by a decrease in both private and public investment. Fiscal deficits increased again after 1998, driven initially by declining public revenues rather than rising public expenditures, which remained stable. Capital expenditures declined, but public debt reached 80 percent of GDP and inflation surged to 8 percent in 2004. During this period, the exchange rate appreciated significantly, ad hoc controls were being implemented in the trade regime, and public banks were effectively bankrupt because of large nonperforming loans.

The reformist government that took office in June 2004 set a major agenda for structural reforms, including (i) simplifying the trade regime and reducing trade tariffs, (ii) improving exchange rate management and floating the currency, (iii) reducing tax rates and simplifying the tax structure, (iv) accelerating privatization, (v) limiting regulatory impediments to business entry and licensing, (vi) streamlining cash and debt management, and (vii) partially adjusting energy prices. Bank support for these reforms was primarily through economic and sector work and reimbursable and other technical assistance, rather than through lending.

The economy responded positively to the reforms. Economic growth accelerated from 4.5 percent in 2005 to 6.8 percent in 2006, largely driven by expanding private investment and aided by a favorable external environment. Exports and imports increased rapidly in 2005 and 2006, and foreign direct investment surged to 5.7 percent of GDP. Private investment increased from 8 percent in 2003 to 11 percent in 2006, and Egypt's stock market was the strongest performer in the region in 2006. The Bank's 2008 *Doing Business* report puts Egypt at the top of the "most improved business climate" list of countries. Privatization in 2005–06 exceeded expectations, and fiscal reforms progressed well, but primary and overall budget deficits remained high. Inflation was contained to single digits, except for fluctuations in 2006 and early 2007. Nevertheless, inflationary pressures from strong domestic demand and rising world food prices persist.

Employment grew 4.6 percent per year between 1998 and 2006, more than the labor force (3.9 percent), leading to a decline in the unemployment rate from 11.7 percent in 1998 to about 8 percent in 2006. An ambitious financial sector reform program was undertaken, supported by the Bank with a development policy loan of $500 million in 2006 (which mobilized a total of $2.2 billion, including other donors), based on a Bank–International Monetary Fund financial sector assessment. The outcome of the first pillar of Bank assistance—promoting higher, more sustainable growth through structural reforms—is rated as moderately satisfactory.

Under the second pillar—*management of water resources, infrastructure, and environment*—progress was good. The Bank has been Egypt's principal partner for three decades in irrigation, pumping and drainage, and community-based rural development, and Bank financed projects account for the renewal and improvement of a large proportion of Egypt's water infrastructure. The Bank has generally been effective in strengthening institutions in Egypt's water resources sector, specifically the Egyptian Public Authority for Agricultural Drainage Projects. The Bank has been less successful with efforts to build institutional capacity at the Mechanical and Electrical Department of the Ministry of Water Resources and Irrigation. It has been instrumental in establishing water users' associations and in the associations' effective involvement in water resources management. The Bank also played a significant role in helping the government implement its Integrated Water Resources Plan. As a result of this long-term engagement, agricultural sector growth and export performances were impressive during the review period. There was no progress, however, in reducing disparities in living standards between Upper and Lower Egypt, even though the Bank's two rural development projects helped improve the standard of living in project areas.

The Bank was absent from the main infrastructure sectors, transport and energy in particular, from fiscal 1999 until fiscal 2004. But it responded quickly to a government request for an Airports Development Project (2004, $335 million), preparing, approving, and beginning disbursement within nine months. The strategic relevance of Bank funding of airports development in Egypt can be questioned on the grounds that the link to poverty reduction is not immediate, yet the Bank's role in these investments helped bring about a fundamental change in Bank-Egypt relations and was followed by another large loan ($270 million) to the power sector in 2006.

The Bank produced a number of analytic and policy-oriented notes in energy, urban transport, railways, telecommunications, and information technology. Airport capacity, as a result of the Bank project, has been significantly increased, thus reducing a potential barrier to tourism. In the energy sector, installed power generation capacity increased and chronic shortages were avoided. Energy reforms are under way, including unbundling and some regulatory strengthening, although there are still many items on the agenda.

Despite recent adjustments, energy prices remain heavily subsidized. The telecommunications sector has been liberalized, allowing private mobile operators to exist and expanding telephone service dramatically. Regarding the environment, the Bank had a small lending program of two loans and carried out several studies; since 2005, air and water quality indicators have started to improve. Outcomes of Bank assistance for this second pillar are rated satisfactory.

For the third pillar—*development of human resources and poverty reduction*—the Bank's assistance strategy was less effective in helping Egypt implement a broad range of social programs. Outcomes are rated as moderately satisfactory, although in the area of gender, disparities have been reduced substantially in education and health during the review period. The Bank's inputs contributed significantly to the present strength of the National Council of Women, a focal point of government's gender efforts. Overall, Bank gender work in Egypt has been a pioneer and a model for the Middle East and North Africa Region.

Education indicators improved over the period under review. Compulsory education was lengthened from eight to nine years; net enrollment ratios in primary education increased by about 9 percent for both boys and girls, to 100 percent and 97 percent, respectively. Enrollment in preparatory school increased much more, to 84 percent for boys and 82 percent for girls. Thus, Egypt made good progress reducing or eliminating remaining problems of access to basic education. Secondary enrollments increased faster, from 2.7 million to 3.2 million. The enrollment rate in secondary education rose from 33 percent to 39 percent.

Although Egypt has achieved considerable progress on indicators in health, nutrition, and population, the Bank's contribution to this has been modest; Egypt did not borrow from the Bank in this area after graduating from IDA. Nevertheless, the Bank financed both targeted interventions—national schistosomiasis control (1992); population in Upper Egypt (1996)—and an innovative Health Sector Reform Program (1998) implemented during the review period with good outcomes. The Bank also provided a series of policy notes on health issues. The government has now requested support from the Bank for health insurance reform.

Egypt made some progress in poverty reduction during the review period, but this has been disappointing overall. The poverty headcount fell from 19.4 percent (1996) to 16.7 percent in 2000, but after a period of slower economic growth, it had risen to 19.6 percent again by 2005. With high GDP growth in 2005 through 2007, it is likely that poverty has fallen, but not necessarily everywhere, and recent figures are not available yet. Upper Egypt has lagged behind Lower Egypt, and both its rural and urban poverty headcounts increased even during the rapid growth of the late 1990s and continued to rise slowly through 2005. The safety net in Egypt consists mainly of subsidies for a small number of basic foodstuffs, particularly bread. These subsidies have lifted some out of poverty, but they do not reach enough of the poor and are not well targeted. Finally, Egypt has made sustained progress toward achieving the Millennium Development Goals related to education, infant and child mortality, maternal mortality, and safe water and sanitation.

In sum, there was progress on many of the objectives of Bank assistance, and the *overall outcome of the Bank's assistance program is rated moderately satisfactory,* although the Bank's contribution to a number of outcomes was often very small in financial terms. However, the Bank produced well-timed and good-quality knowledge products that both government and the donor community respect and that have assisted in policy formulation and reform. In lending, the Bank could have focused more sharply on reducing poverty and inequality, particularly in human development, aiming more of its interventions toward Upper Egypt, where poverty is more pronounced.

The institutional impact of Bank assistance is rated as substantial. The quality of macroeconomic management improved, and progress was made on the institutional reforms in tax administration, customs, and the financial sector. In public financial management, progress was made in transparency and public procurement. The Bank made significant contributions to institutional development in water resources management by helping the government establish small and large-scale water user associations. The present strength of the National Council of Women benefited from the Bank's assistance program.

Although the Bank continued to be overly optimistic regarding Egypt's interest in borrowing or in using policy-based lending in the first part of the period, it did pursue analytic work on poverty and was proactive in improving the performance of its portfolio. It also carried out other good-quality analytic work in many sectors and produced a series of timely policy notes.

The Bank was responsive to the government's request for a rapid appraisal and approval of an airport development project that had not been part of the Bank's strategy. This responsiveness, combined with a buildup of technical expertise in the Cairo office and the ability to harness knowledge from around the world on a wide range of issues of interest to the new reform-minded government, brought about a dramatic shift in the Bank's role in the recent reforms and allowed the Bank to make substantive contributions to the recent progress on structural reforms and economic growth. The risks to development outcomes in Egypt would appear to be moderate at this time, but they remain real in view of the continued presence of large pockets of poverty and the recent unprecedented increase in international food prices.

Future Bank strategy should reflect Egypt's middle-income status by including a flexible lending program and an emphasis on knowledge services, including reimbursable technical assistance. The Bank can further strengthen the recent successful partnership by—

- Improving program focus on *reduction of poverty and inequality*, with a view to identifying direct and indirect interventions that could help reduce income disparities between Upper and Lower Egypt, and including improving targeting of social safety nets through the introduction of a program of conditional cash transfers.
- Giving priority in *analytic work* to macroeconomic analysis, water resources development, infrastructure, and Upper Egypt, and on improving engagement of stakeholders around findings and recommendations.
- In *financial sector and public sector governance,* pursuing lending support for continued financial sector reforms (banking reforms including specialized banks, supervisory framework, capital markets, and nonbanking

financial institutions); and continuing to promote improvements to systems that improve governance and indirectly combat corruption (public financial management, simplification of taxation and business procedures, and information act).

- In *infrastructure and energy,* helping Egypt develop its infrastructure strategy, dealing with issues of public investment and public-private partnerships, and moving beyond capital investments to focus on policy and institutional reforms.

Management Action Record

Management Action Record	
Major monitorable IEG recommendations requiring a response	**Management response**
a) The Bank should increase the assistance program's focus on the persistent issue of *poverty and income disparities*, with a view to identifying direct and indirect interventions that could serve to reduce income disparities, in particular, including improving efficiency and targeting of social safety nets through the introduction of a program of conditional cash transfers. In addition, lending—particularly but not exclusively in human development—should be more focused on Upper Egypt. Much of the knowledge base on poverty and subsidy reform has been built, and it is important to follow up with concrete action.	Management fully agrees with the recommendation to focus on poverty and income disparities, although it also believes that broad-based growth will be key to that effect. This is in line with the Bank's strategy in the period ahead as outlined in the Country Assistance Strategy (CAS) Progress Report that covers the fiscal 2009–11 period. With regard to social protection, management is currently providing support (through technical assistance and South-South exchange of experience) to the design of an in-depth subsidy reform and the introduction of a cash transfer program. With regard to social sectors, management believes that the challenge for the International Bank for Reconstruction and Development (IBRD) is to find innovative and effective ways to provide support and to leverage its comparative advantages, in areas that are not among the government's priorities for borrowing. Knowledge services, including both analytical work and technical assistance (part of which provided as fee-based technical assistance), are critical in that respect. Challenges are similar with regard to Upper Egypt, where IBRD potential lending is also constrained by the government's willingness to borrow. Overall, significant financial resources are available from the government and other sources in the social sectors and for Upper Egypt, and IBRD knowledge services can have a major impact in helping improve the quality of the corresponding investments even in the absence of direct lending.
b) The Bank should be placing greater emphasis than in the past on its *economic and sector work* on macroeconomic analysis, water resource development, infrastructure, and Upper Egypt. The Bank should ensure more systematic dissemination of all economic and sector work.	Management agrees with the recommendation to further strengthen analytical work in these areas and has reflected this in the indicative analytical program for the upcoming years, which is described in the CAS Progress Report that covers the fiscal 2009–11 period.
c) In *financial sector and public sector governance* (i) continue lending support for financial sector reforms, which are incomplete (banking sector reforms including specialized banks, supervisory framework, capital markets, and nonbanking financial institutions), and (ii) continue promoting	Management agrees with the recommendation to strengthen dissemination and consultation processes of the Bank's analytic work and has decided to make specific budget allocations for each piece of analytical work for that purpose. Management agrees with the recommendations in this area and

Management Action Record (*continued*)

Major monitorable IEG recommendations requiring a response	Management response
improvements to systems that indirectly combat corruption (public financial management, simplification of taxation and business procedures, and information act).	is planning to further support these reforms through a combination of lending and analytical work. Specifically, with regard to banking sector reforms, the Bank is (i) working with the government on restructuring the specialized banks (through policy dialogue and technical assistance); (ii) working with both the government and other development partners (especially the European Central Bank, which has taken the lead in this area) on supervision issues; (iii) providing support through both technical assistance (under an Institutional Development Fund) and analytical work for capital markets development; and (iv) expanding its program to the insurance sector (which was part of the Second Financial Sector Reform Development Policy Loan, approved by the Board on May 29, 2008) and microfinance (in close cooperation with the International Finance Corporation [IFC] and Consultative Group to Assist the Poorest). With regard to anticorruption systems, the Bank (i) is finalizing a Country Financial Accountability Assessment and a Report on the Observance of Standards and Codes and is planning to follow up on their findings; (ii) has provided (fee-based) technical assistance for the drafting of a Freedom of Information Act; (iii) is planning to provide further support to help improve Egypt's score on anticorruption indexes, per the government's request; and (iv) is planning to provide technical assistance to the Transparency and Anti-Corruption Commission, also per the government's request.
d) In *infrastructure and energy* (i) assist Egypt in developing its infrastructure strategy dealing with issues of public investment and public-private partnerships and (ii) move beyond capital investments and focus on policy and institutional reforms.	Management agrees with the recommendation to help deal with infrastructure strategy and is planning some analytical work to that effect. Management is also planning to expand support to public-private partnerships (jointly with IFC), through a combination of general advice (on financing schemes, standard risk-sharing arrangements, and so forth), hands-on support to the public-private partnerships unit established in the Ministry of Finance, and specific sectoral advice (especially in the energy sector). Management agrees on the importance of fostering policy and institutional reforms and will continue to work to that effect, including as regards the critical and sensitive issue of energy subsidies. Management does not see a trade-off between such efforts and capital investment lending. Indeed, experience over the recent period suggests that investment operations can be very instrumental in building the type of solid, trust-based sectoral dialogue that is a precondition for the IBRD to be in a position to influence the reform agenda (through separate technical assistance or analytical activities).

Chairperson's Summary: Committee on Development Effectiveness (CODE)

On July 14, 2008, the Informal Subcommittee of the Committee on Development Effectiveness (CODE) considered the Country Assistance Evaluation (CAE) prepared by the Independent Evaluation Group (IEG) on the Arab Republic of Egypt.

Summary of the Egypt CAE

The CAE reviewed the outcomes of the Bank's assistance between fiscal 1999 and fiscal 2007. During that period, Bank assistance to Egypt was guided by three Country Assistance Strategies (CASs). IEG found that the focus of the CASs was relevant and consistent with the key development objectives of the government. The country achieved good progress in macroeconomic management, financial sector reform, and private sector development. In the area of poverty reduction and inequality, the progress was uneven and sometimes disappointing. Therefore, the overall outcome of the Bank's assistance program is rated as moderately satisfactory, and the institutional impact of Bank assistance is rated as substantial. Although the Bank financial support was modest, with relatively little lending, its analytical work and poverty advice made significant contributions to reforms and policy changes across many sectors. IEG recommended that future Bank strategy should reflect Egypt's middle-income status by including a flexible lending program and putting strong emphasis on knowledge services. In addition, IEG recommendations included (i) improving program focus on reduction of poverty and inequality and helping reduce some regional disparities; (ii) giving priority in analytic work to macroeconomic analysis, water resource development, infrastructure, and Upper Egypt; (iii) pursuing lending support for continued financial sector reforms and promoting investments to systems that improve governance and indirectly combat corruption; and (iv) assisting Egypt in developing its infrastructure strategy and moving beyond capital investments to policy and institutional reforms in infrastructure and energy sectors.

Management's Comments

In general, management agreed with the IEG findings and recommendations. At the same time, it stressed the need for evaluating outcomes of both the International Bank for Reconstruction and Development (IBRD)/the International Development Association (IDA) and International Finance Corporation (IFC) programs, especially because over the CAE period IFC was active, with loans and investments totaling $842 million across a diversified portfolio. Management also highlighted the Bank's role in helping the country develop and implement a broad range of social sector programs through its solid economic and sector work and active cooperation with other donors. In this regard, it was emphasized that the Bank's influence in social sectors cannot be measured only by the size of its lending program. Management also fully agreed with the IEG recommendation to focus on poverty and income disparities and believed that broad-based growth will be a key factor in this regard. Management noted that most of IEG's recommendations were reflected in the most recent CAS Progress Report.

Comments from the Government

The government commended IEG for its efforts in preparing such a comprehensive and precise CAE and expressed its consensus with all recommendations, especially those aimed at the reduction of poverty and income disparities, human development, and focus on the environmental, social, and infrastructure sectors. At the same time, the government emphasized the importance of reflecting Egypt's middle-income status by including a flexible lending program in future Bank strategy. It pointed out that the Bank in Egypt should be a knowledge institution rather than a financial one and thus should share its international experiences and best practices in debt-servicing, financial and social reforms, building good governance, and adopting anticorruption measures.

The representative of the constituency that includes Egypt overall supported the CAE findings and recommendations and emphasized country ownership as a key element for success. He highlighted significant achievements during the CAE period, that is, improvements in macroeconomic management, reduction of fiscal deficit, acknowledgment of Egypt as a top reformer in the 2008 *Doing Business* report, significant improvements in portfolio performance, increased volume of IFC investments, and success in the implementation of the first phase of an ambitious financial sector reform. He also underlined the government's constant attention to the issues of poverty reduction and regional inequality, but noted that borrowing from the Bank for social sectors was time consuming and costly. He stressed that currently Egypt faces the challenges of high oil and food prices, inflationary pressures, and rising poverty and needs the Bank's knowledge services as well as investment lending.

Main Conclusions and the Next Steps

The subcommittee welcomed the informative CAE and, overall, supported the IEG findings and recommendations. Members commended the government for the remarkable economic growth, although they expressed concerns about the persistent poverty and inequality in the country. To this end, the need for expanding the Bank's presence in social sectors was emphasized by several speakers. A member stressed the importance of having a joint evaluation of IBRD/IDA and IFC assistance. Some members sought information on donor coordination, especially due to the fact that the Bank's financial assistance to Egypt provides only 4 percent of the total official development assistance. Speakers raised questions about the applicability of Egypt's experience in other countries of the Region and emphasized the importance of flexibility in future lending and analytical and advisory assistance (AAA). Additionally, a speaker remarked on the need for the Bank to further mainstream gender in its work. The CAE will be publicly disclosed. The CAS Progress Report will be discussed by the Board of Executive Directors on July 17, 2008.

The following issues were raised.

Economic growth, poverty, and inequality

Commending Egyptian authorities for the remarkable economic growth and structural reforms, members also expressed concerns that this growth has not resulted in poverty reduction and asked about the main reasons for that. *Management explained that in Egypt the sectors contributing to the economic growth are not labor intensive. In addition, management clarified that starting in 2004 the methodology for poverty measurement has been improved and the poverty rates are measured more accurately.* They also noted the need to underpin the technical assistance with lending for reducing social and regional inequalities and asked about future Bank plans in this area. In this connection, a member wondered whether the analytical work and advisory services would have a significant impact on poverty without substantial investments. *IEG explained that as the evaluation shows, even with low amounts of lending, the Bank can influence poverty reduction through good donor coordination and solid AAA that sets out a framework for reforms in the country. In addition, management clarified that the government requested Bank support in strengthening social safety nets and designing a conditional cash transfer program aimed at reducing poverty and inequality. Management also praised the role of South-South cooperation in the areas of subsidy reform and improving targeting of social safety nets.* Another member recommended tackling poverty through sound countercyclical fiscal policies and provision of adequate diagnostic tools. *IEG responded that the current size of the fiscal deficit does not allow the government to implement countercyclical fiscal policies to address social issues.*

Coordination with development partners

Noting the Bank's modest assistance to Egypt relative to total official development assistance, members sought a detailed analysis of coordination with other development partners, including division of labor between the Bank and the major donors. *IEG explained that the evaluation focused on key development partners, that is, the International Monetary Fund (IMF), the U.S. Agency for International Development, the European Union, and the African Development Bank (AfDB). The Bank played a significant role in donor coordination: it cooperated with the IMF on the financial sector review as well as with the U.S. Agency for International Development and AfDB on the financial sector reforms and social programs. Management added that a donor assistance group comprising the European Commission, the Bank, the IMF, the AfDB, the United Nations Development Programme, and the development agencies of Japan, Germany, and the Netherlands was established to strengthen coordination.* Members recommended that the Bank be more engaged with other donors and raised questions about donor harmonization efforts in the infrastructure sector.

Airport development project and flexible lending

Some members commended the Bank for its responsiveness and fast preparation of the Airport Development Project, although one member felt that the CAE overstated the importance of the project in revitalizing the Bank-country relations. *Management agreed that the turning point for this revitalization was the appointment of a reform-oriented government rather than the preparation of the project. However, the project experience was helpful in convincing the counterparts that the Bank could be responsive, quick, reliable, and flexible in its investment lending.* In this connection, members asked about the ways of improving Bank's operational strategy and increasing flexibility and alignment of lending.

Social sectors and environment

Members remarked on the Bank's limited lending for health, education, and environment. A member noted the moderately satisfactory outcomes for environment and wondered how interventions in the water resources and infrastructure were taken into account. He emphasized the importance of work on environmental issues, especially because the Bank had launched the Sustainable Infrastructure Action Plan that called for streamlining of these issues. *IEG responded that despite the relatively small size of lending (that is, one project in the amount of $20 million), the Bank has provided solid economic and sector work and cooperated with other donors, using its comparative advantage. Management added that such strategy helped mobilize $200 million in financing from the European Union and the government of Japan.* A member sought further information about achievements in the quality of education.

Macroeconomic management and financial sector

In general, members commended the authorities for the success in macroeconomic management, tax reform, and fiscal debt reduction but noted that further progress in these areas is required. To this end, the importance of implementing reforms on both the expenditure and the revenue sides was underlined. A member emphasized the need for technical assistance in strengthening tax policy and sought further information about the Bank's role in the tax sector. A comment about over-reliance on IMF advice was made. In addition, members raised questions about the impact of financial sector reforms on poverty reduction.

Infrastructure

Members welcomed the re-engagement of the Bank in the infrastructure sector and broadly concurred with the general thrust of IEG recommendations, emphasizing the importance of structural reforms in this area. In this regard, a question about the Bank's future strategy in infrastructure was raised. *IEG clarified that since fiscal 2004 the Bank has also actively supported the government in infrastructure through investment lending. IEG recommends focusing on policy issues and institutional reforms in this sector.*

Gender

A member noted the progress made by Egypt in improving gender equality and wondered how the Bank could most effectively expand on this success. *IEG clarified that the Bank provided substantial AAA and economic and sector work and helped establish the National Council of Women. Management added that future work in gender will focus on economic empowerment of women and on strengthening their participation in the labor market.*

Strengthening governance and combating corruption

A member noted the economic, social, and political importance of fighting corruption. *IEG clarified that indirect measures (that is, through private sector development, privatization, public sector reform, better tax policy and public expenditure management, and financial sector reform) contributed to better governance, and this approach had been used in Egypt.*

Replication of Egypt's experience

A member wondered what aspects of the Bank's strategy in Egypt would be replicable for the other countries in the Middle East and North Africa Region. *Management responded that the initiatives that could be replicated include support to public-private partnerships, particularly in the water sector; financial sector reform; and improving business climate.*

Jiayi Zou, Chairperson

Chapter 1

The Bank has projects in the agriculture, infrastructure, social protection, health, and environment sectors—all of which are making a difference throughout the country. Photo courtesy of Victor Orozco, World Bank Group.

Introduction and Country Background

This Country Assistance Evaluation (CAE) reviews the World Bank Group's assistance to the Arab Republic of Egypt from fiscal 1999 through fiscal 2007. Bank assistance (International Development Association [IDA]/International Bank for Reconstruction and Development [IBRD]) over the period fiscal 1991 to fiscal 1998 was covered by a previous CAE in 2000 (IEG 2000; see box 1.1 at the end of this chapter).

Egypt is a country of more than 74 million people. It has a per capita income of $1,580 (2006 gross national income [GNI], Atlas method) and occupies a crucial position in the geopolitics of the Middle East. Less than 5 percent of Egypt's total 1 million square kilometers of land area is settled and cultivated. Most of the rest is uninhabitable desert—more than 97 percent of the population lives in the narrow strip of the highly fertile Nile valley and its delta.

There are major differences in poverty and inequality across regions in Egypt, with the highest poverty in Upper Egypt (south), both rural and urban, and the lowest in metropolitan areas and Lower Egypt (north). Successive governments have consistently shown strong concern for social equity and political stability. This is reflected in the significant public resources that have been allocated to social spending. In addition to domestic resources, Egypt has had large external financial assistance flows, mostly in the form of grants, mainly provided by the United States, the European Union (EU), and other Arab countries.

In 1991 Egypt began an ambitious program of stabilization and structural reform, supported by donors. The first phase, up to 1996, consisted of fiscal deficit control, exchange rate reform, liberalization of most prices and interest rates, import tariff reductions, and initiation of public enterprise privatizations. With effective fiscal adjustment and sound monetary policy management, inflation was brought down from higher than 20 percent in 1991 to below 10 percent in 1995.

Macroeconomic stabilization led to strong recovery. Gross domestic product (GDP) growth rose from the stagnation of the early 1990s to 4.7 percent in 1995 and continued its upward momentum into 1996 (figure 1.1). From being one of the most heavily indebted countries in the world at the end of the 1980s, Egypt reduced its debt-to-GDP ratio to 60 percent by 1995. This was in part a result of the 1991 Paris Club agreement of external debt restructuring as well as of debt forgiveness by the United States and Gulf countries.

Figure 1.1: Egypt: GDP Growth Rates, 1990–2007

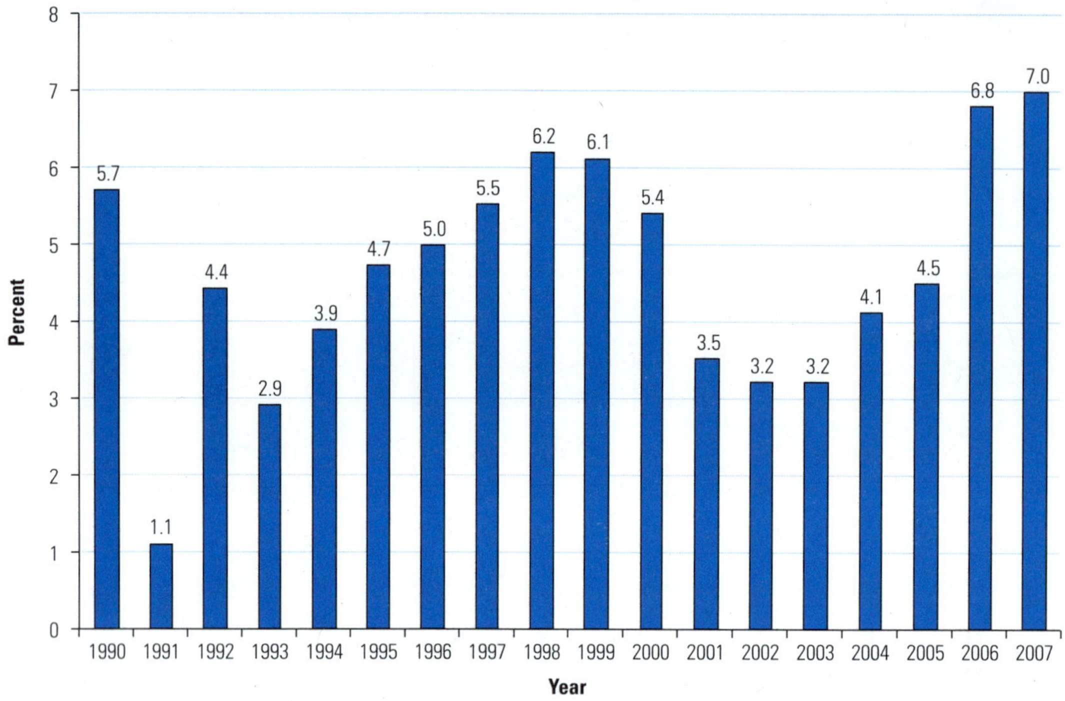

Source: World Bank and IMF data.

In 1996, the government began to speed up privatization and pursue other reforms more aggressively: In less than two years it sold its controlling interest in 65 companies and minority interest in another 16, removed most quantitative restrictions on imports and reduced tariffs, decontrolled many rents, liberalized investment procedures, passed a new investment law, and undertook financial sector and tax reforms. Results over the next several years were good: Private investment grew to almost 13 percent of GDP, compared with less than 10 percent in the early 1990s; growth was 5.3 percent per annum between 1995 and 2000; and inflation continued to decline to less than 4 percent in 1998. Egypt should be given considerable credit for carrying out fundamental reforms in the 1990s without igniting unrest and for maintaining sound macroeconomic management and performance in the face of the financial crisis that hit many emerging markets in the 1997–99 period.

Between 2001 and 2003, Egypt's GDP growth rate slowed, averaging only 3.2 percent per annum. Contributing to this slowdown was the vulnerability of services to destabilizing factors associated with the region (such as September 11 and the Iraq war) as well as a decline in the Organisation for Economic Co-operation and Development growth. Private investment declined from 13 percent of GDP in 1998 to 8 percent in 2003. This low level was a cause for concern because it is widely believed that private investment should serve as the main engine of growth and employment.

Fiscal deficits began rising after 1998, following a long period of improvement. Disaggregated fiscal accounts show that fiscal deficits were driven initially by declining public revenues rather than rising public expenditures. Total public expenditures remained stable at 30 percent of GDP between 1999 and 2003, while revenues declined from 23 percent to 20 percent. The low buoyancy of revenues during the 1990s indicates that structural weaknesses—narrow tax base and inefficient tax administration—were at work. The net public debt level reached 82 percent of GDP and inflation surged to 11.7 percent in 2004. Unemployment rose in early 2000 and reached about 11 percent in 2003. The young and women, in particular, suffered the highest unemployment rates.

The government that came to power in July 2004 embarked on a far-reaching reform program. A new cabinet led by Prime Minister Ahmed Nazif, first appointed in 2004, was reappointed in December 2005 following parliamentary elections. The economic team was also reinstated, reaffirming the government's commitment to economic reform. The election resulted in a parliamentary majority for the ruling National Democratic Party, with members of the Muslim Brotherhood—who ran as independents—winning about 20 percent of the seats in parliament.

Since 2004, reforms have given the private sector a greater role. Correction of the exchange rate and its management eliminated the distortions generated by a parallel market premium. The tariff structure was simplified and the import-weighted average tariff reduced from 14 to 7 percent. Tax rates were lowered and the base broadened. Privatization has been revived, and significant progress has been achieved in the implementation of the financial sector reform program.

Economic growth surged to a 20-year high of 7 percent in 2006. The external sector remains an important engine of growth, but the expansion has become more broad based, with construction and services now increasing at a healthy rate. Privatization in 2005 and 2006 exceeded expectations, and reforms in the fiscal area have prepared the ground for fiscal consolidation to go forward. The privatization of the fourth largest state bank (Bank of Alexandria) was completed in early 2007. Private investment steadily increased from 8 percent in 2003 to 11 percent of GDP in 2006. Egypt's stock market was the strongest performer in the region in 2006. Employment has grown impressively: 4.6 percent annually between 1998 and 2006, more than the labor force growth of 3.9 percent or population growth of 2 percent.

Rapid growth in incomes and employment in the late 1990s led to a drop in poverty for the first time since the early 1980s, to less than 16.7

Table 1.1: Egypt: Social Indicators, 1996–2005/06

Indicator	1996	2005
Extreme poverty (%)	2.0	3.8
Poverty rate (%)	19.4	19.6
$1/day	7.0	3.4
$2/day	57.0	42.8
Life expectancy (M/F)	65/69	68/72
Infant mortality (per 1,000)	44	33
Maternal mortality (per 100,000)	84	63
Education		
Gross primary enrollment	100	100
Gross secondary enrollment	74	86

Sources: Egyptian Central Agency for Public Mobilization and Statistics (CAPMAS) and World Bank World Development Indicators.

percent of the population in 1999–2000 from higher than 19.4 percent in 1995–96. It rose again through 2005 to its baseline level during a period of slower growth in the early 2000s. With the more rapid economic growth realized from 2005 to 2007, it is reasonable to assume that the poverty headcount has fallen again. The proportion of the population living on $1 and $2 per day diminished between 1995–96 and 2005. Further, although Egypt has higher poverty rates than the middle-income countries in the Middle East and North Africa Region, it fares better than richer countries such as the Philippines and Indonesia and—in terms of extreme poverty—better than Brazil and Mexico. Most of the poor remain concentrated in Upper Egypt, particularly in the rural region, where the poverty rate was 39 percent in 2005.

During the past 10 years, human development indicators have improved substantially in Egypt (see table 1.1). Infant and maternal mortality rates have declined, while gross secondary school enrollment has increased substantially. Moreover, many social indicators are better in Egypt than in countries with comparable income levels. Life expectancy increased from 65 and 69 years in 1996 for males and females, respectively, to 68 and 72 years by 2005, thus surpassing the Region average. Egypt has made sustained progress toward achieving the Millennium Development Goals related to water and sanitation, infant and child mortality, and maternal mortality. However, though diminishing over time, regional disparities in education and health indicators remain large. In 2005, adult illiteracy was 43.5 percent in Upper Egypt and 35.1 percent in Lower Egypt.

Box 1.1: IEG Country Assistance Evaluation (2000)

In January 2000, the Independent Evaluation Group (IEG) completed a CAE for Egypt. The report focused in particular on the period between 1990 and 1998, although it included an overview of Bank assistance to Egypt since 1950. The following is a summary of the report's key findings and recommendations.

- Egypt had done a commendable job of implementing significant structural reform and sustaining sound macroeconomic policies, leading to strong growth without major social unrest in the 1990–98 period.
- Some social indicators, such as child malnutrition and life expectancy, improved markedly. Others, including literacy (particularly among women) and infant mortality, although improved, had not achieved gains commensurate with increased access to social services.
- The Bank's role in Egypt had been modest, although it was actively involved in the early 1990s in supporting structural adjustment and in helping Egypt with major debt rescheduling.
- An important gap in Bank assistance was the absence of work on poverty.
- Because of large amounts of concessional funding available to Egypt, IEG recommended that the Bank forge closer partnerships and cofinancing arrangements with other donors.
- IEG also recommended that the Bank broaden the scope of its dialogue to cover poverty, private sector development, the financial sector, and governance.
- IEG recommended that the Bank continue to lend in areas where the government is interested and where the Bank has had positive results, such as in irrigation and drainage.
- IEG noted that the subsequent Country Assistance Strategy needed to propose clear guidelines to link the administrative budget to the size and complexity of the portfolio and the likely effective demand by the Egyptian government for the Bank's lending and nonlending services.

Source: IEG 2000.

Chapter 2

Men gather at a canal; water resources management has always been one of the Bank's main areas of support.
Photo by Ray Witlin, courtesy of the World Bank Photo Library.

The Bank's Strategy and Assistance Program

Overview of a Long Relationship

Egypt's view of the Bank has always been influenced by its earliest interactions. For more than three years starting in 1953, the Bank actively considered financing the High Dam at Aswan. Bank financing was contingent on grant financing from the United States and Great Britain, and when those two countries backed out in 1956, so did the Bank. The High Dam, one of the largest ever built, was ultimately financed with Soviet money.

Within a week of the withdrawal of the American and British offer of financing, Egypt nationalized the foreign-owned Suez Canal Company. The Bank played a key role in helping to settle the claims for compensation arising from this, which then opened the way for the Bank to make its first loan to Egypt in 1959, to the Suez Canal Authority for improvements to the canal. Nevertheless, in the minds of some government officials and Egyptian citizens, the Bank's failure to finance the High Dam left a certain mistrust and a view that the Bank is unduly influenced by important shareholders.

Until 1990, the Bank concentrated on project lending. In 1991, however, Egypt sought debt relief from the Paris Club, which conditioned debt forgiveness on progress under a reform program formulated in conjunction with the Bank and the International Monetary Fund (IMF). The Bank reached agreement with the government in 1991 for a Structural Adjustment Loan ($300 million), but Egypt proved reluctant to meet the conditions for release of the second tranche, which included privatization; reducing import bans; price liberalization in industry, energy, and agriculture; and the establishment of holding companies. However, because it needed the approval of the Bank and IMF to obtain debt forgiveness, the government eventually did the minimum necessary to meet the tranche release conditions, although it never drew on the tranche and half the loan amount was canceled. Egypt was subsequently granted debt relief. After this experience, Egypt did not agree to policy-based lending for 15 years, until fiscal 2006.

Because of the pressures from external institutions to carry out reforms, Egypt wanted to avoid becoming heavily indebted again. For some years after this Structural Adjustment Loan/Paris Club experience, Egypt limited its borrowing from all sources, including the World Bank. The ready availability of large amounts of grant funding allowed Egypt to finance investment projects and avail itself of external advice without needing to use relatively expensive Bank funds, having to deal with Bank conditionality, or having to incur high transaction costs. During the 1990s, the government allowed the Bank to prepare several projects in some detail, which were then funded by other, lower-cost funds. It was a difficult period for Bank assistance in Egypt.

During 1999–2007, there were two distinct periods. Once Egypt graduated from IDA in June 1999, a period of transition followed. Egypt moved from being a blend (IDA/IBRD) country to an IBRD-only country. Many large donors were active, offering grants, low interest rates, and subsidized loans, and Egypt was understandably reluctant to borrow only on IBRD terms. For about half the period under review, until fiscal 2004, there were no large loans outside of irrigation and drainage, although the Bank had an intensive dialogue, on two separate occasions, on a proposed policy-based loan (of some $500 million) that never materialized. The government had serious concerns about the risk of economic and political shocks that the proposed reforms would bring about. The Bank focused on cleaning up the portfolio and carried out a few economic studies.

In 2003 and 2004 two things happened to change the Bank-Egypt relationship. In 2003, the government asked the Bank to support airport development and to do it as quickly as possible; the Bank responded to this request and rapidly appraised and approved a large project. Second, a new reform-minded government launched a wide-ranging program of reforms and sought Bank advice and financial support for the structural reform process. By 2004 a new era had been ushered in: the Bank and the Egyptian government had established policy dialogue in a wide range of sectors; shifted to much higher lending, including development policy loans (DPLs); carried out analytic work in areas where the government had been uncooperative in the past, such as poverty; and had a broader mix of instruments, including reimbursable technical assistance (TA).

Bank Assistance Strategy

Between fiscal 1999 and 2007, Bank operations were guided by three country assistance strategies (CASs), approved in fiscal 1997, 2001, and 2005. Although there was variance across the documents, the dominant and consistent themes were promotion of higher, more sustainable economic growth through structural reforms; development of water resources, infrastructure, and environment; and development of human resources and poverty reduction (see box 2.1). Given the problems facing Egypt, each of these themes was relevant. The Bank strategy was also consistent with the key development objectives and targets of the government of Egypt, as expressed in the fourth and fifth five-year plans, covering the 1997–2007 period. Specifically, Egypt sought high and sustainable growth and the alleviation of poverty and attenuation of income disparities.

The CASs tried to be responsive to the country's perceived needs, but the assistance strategies in 1997 and 2001 in particular suffered from consistent overoptimism. Recognizing the availability of large grants from other donors to Egypt, the 1997 CAS focused on nonlending services, the potential for guarantees, and synergies with the International Finance Corporation (IFC) in private sector development. It specified four areas of Bank support, but its proposed lending program was relatively unfocused and included support for preservation of cultural heritage, thermal power, transport pollution control, and port sector reform. It specified indicators for monitoring results, but many were not easily monitorable in the timeframe of the CAS. Risk assessment was adequate, but that CAS remained unrealistic about three things: the role the Bank could play in supporting Egypt's reform program, the government's interest in borrowing, and the government's willingness to have the Bank carry out any poverty analysis.

The 2001 CAS tried to draw on lessons of experience and on the previous CAE findings. Accordingly, it proposed relatively modest lending levels and foresaw a focus on interventions

Box 2.1: The Evaluation Framework

Pillar One: Promoting Higher, More Sustainable Growth through Structural Reforms

- Maintaining macroeconomic stability and improving public sector governance
- Trade policy and administration reform
- Private sector development and improvement in the regulatory environment
- Financial sector reform

Pillar Two: Management of Water Resources, Infrastructure, and Environment

- Improving water resources management, agriculture, and rural development
- Enhancing civil aviation, telecommunications, and energy infrastructure
- Strengthening environmental management

Pillar Three: Development of Human Resources and Poverty Reduction

- Reducing gender disparities
- Improving access and quality of education services
- Improving health status of the population
- Strengthening social safety nets and subsidy program

Source: World Bank.

where (i) the government's commitment to carrying out projects was clear (as opposed to proceeding to prepare projects where there was a substantial risk of cancellation), (ii) Bank projects had had good outcomes, (iii) the Bank could bring the experience of other countries to guide Egypt's policy reforms, and (iv) Bank lending could be a catalyst for mobilizing additional financing.

The over-riding theme of the 2001 CAS was appropriately poverty reduction. However, even though many planned interventions, both lending and nonlending, were consistent with that objective, others, such as support for higher education and information technology, were included under the very general objective of "indirect poverty reduction." Those interventions could describe *any* Bank intervention and thus resulted in another wide-ranging set of proposed activities.

The 2001 CAS had clear triggers for moving from a base case to high case lending scenario and a number of outcome indicators for the Bank's program. But despite years of the Bank experiencing unfulfilled lending targets in Egypt, the 2001 CAS again proved overly optimistic. The Bank was unable to deliver the program it had planned, in terms of the number of projects approved, use of policy-based lending, carrying out a broader social development agenda other than small education loans, and—if it had not been for one large unplanned project—the amount of lending.

The 2005 CAS was prepared at a very different time. A new government had embarked on a far-reaching reform program, with bold measures already initiated and plans for others announced. The objectives were well aligned with the government's own program and covered three important areas: private sector development, enhancing the provision of public services, and promoting equity. It was a results-based strategy, with monitoring indicators specified; it was also a thorough risk analysis, covering both external and domestic risks.

In view of the improved reform environment, a base case lending program of $500 million a year was proposed over the fiscal 2006–09 period (three times higher than under the previous CAS), with a high case lending scenario of $700 million per annum, including two quick-disbursing policy loans to support financial sector reforms. The triggers for moving to the high case were implementation of substantive financial sector reforms and a financing plan for meeting the total funding needs of the financial sector reform program that showed at least 10 percent funding to be obtained from non-debt-creating sources. These triggers were quickly met, and the Bank moved to the high case scenario in fiscal 2006.

Overview of Lending

The Bank has always had a relatively small role in assistance to Egypt compared to other donors, particularly the U.S. Agency for International Development (USAID) and, more recently, the EU. During 1999–2005 (latest year for which information is available), Bank disbursement was less than 4 percent of the $16.1 billion gross official financial flows to Egypt. For concessional aid alone, the Bank's share was even smaller, representing only 1 percent of total official development assistance. Between fiscal 1999 and 2007, the Bank made commitments of $2.1 billion for 18 investment credits and one policy-based (adjustment) loan, with wide yearly fluctuations in both commitments and disbursements (see figure 2.1).

A total of $550 million was committed in fiscal 1999 alone, most of which was on IDA terms. It is clear from the pattern of commitments that the Bank wanted to commit as much of the country's IDA allocation as it could before Egypt's graduation. For example, a $300 million loan (Private Sector and Agriculture Development Project) was extended during the last year before graduation. That loan was then canceled in its entirety four years later because the government was not interested in carrying out the conditions and reforms required by the project. There was a marked slowdown in lending in the four years after Egypt's graduation from IDA.

Although the 2001 CAS aimed to be more realistic than its predecessor, only three of the eight loans proposed in the CAS were approved by June 2004, totaling $68 million against a planned $450 million. But the late addition of a large fiscal 2004 loan ($335 million) for an airport, to stimulate growth by eliminating bottlenecks at airports and boosting tourism, brought total approvals close to target. This project was not part of the CAS. In addition, negotiations over a policy-based loan ($500 million) following the adverse impacts of the events of September 11, 2001, revealed continued government reluctance to engage in borrowing with conditionality on reforms. With the improvement in the balance of payments,

Figure 2.1: IDA/IBRD Commitments and Disbursements, Fiscal 1999–2007 ($ million)

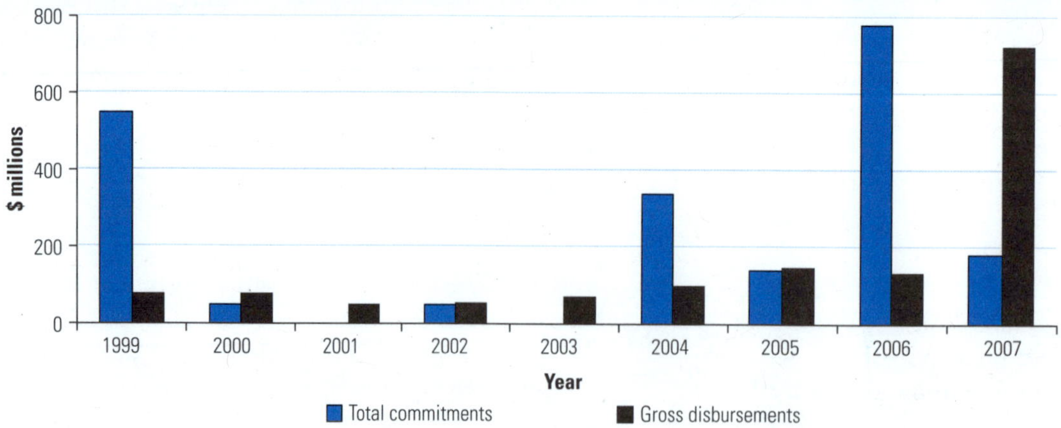

Source: World Bank internal database and World Bank Client Connection.

this policy-based loan was dropped. Thus, although actual lending approached proposed lending, the 2001 CAS proved again to be overly optimistic on lending levels and on the ability of the Bank to engage the government on reforms.

In contrast, by the time of the 2005 CAS, the government was engaged in wide-ranging and deep reforms. As noted earlier, the Bank was able to shift to its high case lending scenario in the middle of fiscal 2006 and provided support for structural reforms with a $500 million DPL, the first to Egypt in 15 years for the financial sector. Lending commitments progressed in fiscal 2006 and fiscal 2007 along the lines of projections in the 2005 CAS. Only one planned operation, the Social Fund for Development (SFD) Project, was dropped in the first two years of implementation. Thus it appears that Bank strategy in that CAS reflected the willingness of the government to borrow from the IBRD and to engage the Bank in its reform efforts.

Sector distribution

Slight changes were made in the composition of lending from the previous CAE period to this, as shown in table 2.1. These involved a shift from an emphasis on the social sectors and, to a lesser extent, economic policy to a greater focus on both infrastructure and structural reforms. The largest share of lending was allocated to the second pillar in both periods, mainly for water resources management (irrigation and drainage), rural finance, and rural development projects; this share increased from 51 percent to 66 percent. Given the overwhelming importance of efficient use of the Nile River waters for the country, this is appropriate.

In addition, the Bank appears to have a good dialogue in water resources management. Two big projects, the Airports Development Project and the El Tebbin Power Project, account for most of the rest of Bank support under the second pillar. Only one loan in the environment sector (Second Pollution Abatement Project) was

Table 2.1: IDA/IBRD Commitments by Pillar and Sector Board

	Fiscal 1990–98			Fiscal 1999–2007		
Sector	**Number of loans**	**Commitment ($ millions)**	**%**	**Number of loans**	**Commitment* ($ millions)**	**%**
Pillar I	2	309	18.0	2	537	26.0
Economic policy	1	300	17.1	—	—	—
Financial and private sector development	—	—	—	2	537	25.5
Public sector governance	1	9	0.5	—	—	—
Pillar II	12	895	51.0	10	1,387	66.0
Energy and mining	3	339	19.3	1	260	12.3
Environment	1	35	2.0	1	20	1.0
Water resources/rural development	6	389	22.1	7	772	36.7
Transport	1	2	0.1	1	335	15.9
Urban development	1	130	7.4	—	—	—
Pillar III	8	555	32.0	6	181	9.0
Education	3	161	9.2	4	126	6.0
Health, nutrition, and population	3	134	7.6	—	—	—
Social protection	2	260	14.8	2	55	2.6
Total	22	1,759	100.0	18	2,105	100.0

Source: World Bank internal database as of September 25, 2007.
Note: Percentage totals for pillars are rounded.

Figure 2.2: Percent of Projects at Risk, Fiscal 1999–2007

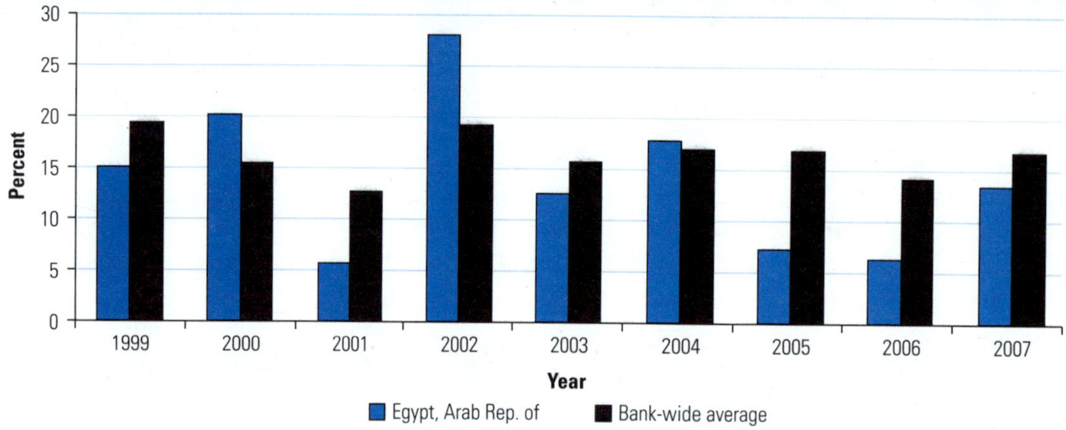

Source: World Bank internal database.

approved between fiscal 1999 and fiscal 2007, although two others were under implementation during the CAE period; together these represented a small share of total lending.

Under the first pillar, sustainable growth through structural reforms, the Bank allocated a quarter of lending resources. This included a financial sector DPL and an innovative mortgage finance project loan, which provided long-term local currency lending for residential housing. The share of this pillar was smaller in the fiscal 1990–98 period, covering only the Structural Adjustment Loan I.

Lending under pillar three, human development and poverty reduction, reflects in part Egypt's transition from an IDA-eligible low-income country to a lower-middle-income country. In the first period (fiscal 1990–98), there was lending to all social sectors. The government was generally unwilling to borrow for social sectors in the CAE period. The share of the third pillar in total lending declined from 32 percent to less than 10 percent. One exception was in education and training, but Bank lending there shifted to emphasize the higher levels of the system, with several small projects (averaging $25–$30 million per project). The last two loans to social protection were extended in fiscal 1999. The government dropped a proposed fourth project using the SFD at a later stage of preparation.

Portfolio performance

The quality of the active portfolio improved gradually over the CAE period. At the end of fiscal 2002, 5 of 18 projects were in problem status and Egypt was on the Bank-wide watch list for countries with commitment at risk above 33 percent. Through efforts to build implementation capacity, restructure projects, cancel unused amounts, and close IDA projects, the Egypt portfolio improved dramatically: projects at risk decreased to 13 percent of the portfolio (from greater than 33 percent); the disbursement ratio increased from 7 percent to greater than 25 percent, better than the Regional and Bank-wide averages on both counts (figures 2.2 and 2.3), and project effectiveness delays were markedly reduced.

In fiscal 1994–98, the cost in Egypt of dropped projects as a portion of direct costs (lending, economic and sector work, supervision) was almost two and a half times the Bank's average:

Figure 2.3: Disbursement Ratios, Fiscal 1999–2007

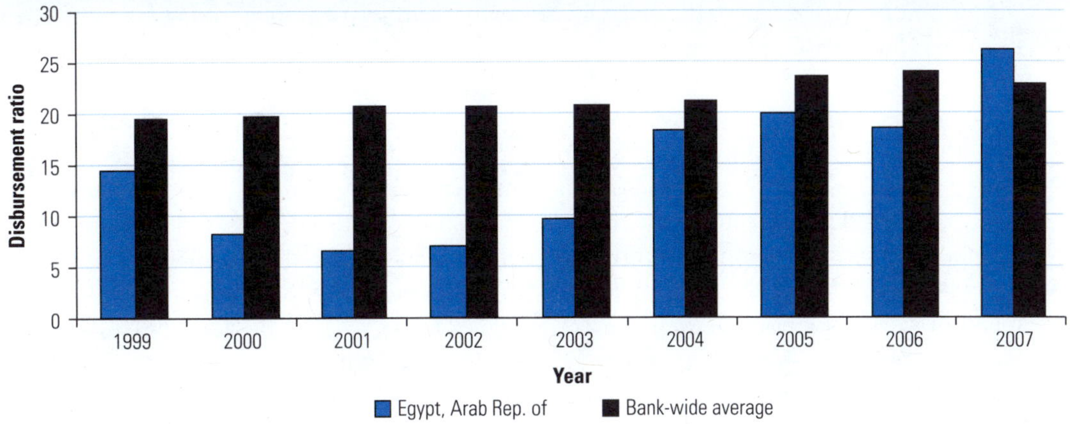

Source: World Bank internal database.

a large number of projects were dropped late in the project cycle, after considerable resources had been spent. The dropped and canceled projects reflected the Bank's desire to lend even when the government was reluctant to borrow, particularly on IBRD terms, and the ease with which the government had been able to find grant funds. Consistent with both the previous CAE recommendation and the CAS target, the Bank successfully reduced the number and cost of dropped projects in the current CAE period.

According to Independent Evaluation Group (IEG) data, 90 percent of the projects that exited the portfolio between 1999 and 2007 had satisfactory outcomes by value, compared with 81 percent in the Middle East and North Africa

Table 2.2: IEG Aggregate Ratings (by project exit year), Fiscal 1999–2007

	Total evaluated		Outcome % satisfactory		Inst development impact % substantial		Sustainability % likely	
Country	**$ million**	**Number**	**$ million**	**Number**	**$ million**	**Number**	**$ million**	**Number**
Egypt	904.3	20	89.7	83.3	51	46.7	63.5	73.3
Algeria	550.8	19	62.5	68.4	41	30.8	49.7	50.0
Indonesia	8,016.3	89	66.8	65.5	31	35.4	51.4	44.3
Morocco	1,698.6	30	63.2	73.3	34	30.0	74.7	88.9
Tunisia	1,579.1	26	95.9	92.3	55	68.0	96.8	95.8
Turkey	5,966.7	34	92.9	90.9	66	48.4	90.8	78.6
Region	7,320.0	189	81.1	74.3	45	37.6	80.7	72.1
World Bank	163,533.0	2,367	80.4	76.1	54	49.6	80.6	73.2

Source: World Bank internal database as of December 19, 2007.

Region and 80 percent Bank-wide. Only two projects were rated unsatisfactory during this period: the Private Sector and Agriculture Development Project and the Private Sector Tourism Infrastructure Project.

Institutional development impact was also better than the Region average and consistent with Bank-wide averages: 51 percent of operations were considered to have substantial institutional development impact, compared with 45 percent in the Region and 54 percent Bank-wide. Sustainability, however, was not as strong: it was considered likely for 64 percent of projects by value, much lower than the Middle East and North Africa Region and Bank-wide averages of 81 percent.

Analytical and Advisory Activities

The CASs presented a coherent and integrated nonlending program that fit well with the strategic agenda for Bank involvement in Egypt and took into account the limited lending opportunities. The focus on poverty analysis and poverty reduction, as well as on enhancing the intellectual underpinnings for Bank lending activities in numerous sectors was appropriate. With the exception of a poverty assessment planned for fiscal 1999 (which was not carried out until the government agreed to it, a number of years later), most of the planned analytical products were delivered in the CAE period. In the early part of the period under review, the Bank allocated as much as 45 percent of its administrative budget to supervision, but once the portfolio was restructured, supervision requirements decreased and nonlending services increased to about one-third of the administrative budget. This was comparable with the Middle East and North Africa Region and Bank-wide averages.

There was a significant gap in poverty analysis during the previous CAE period. After a long period in which the Bank had a limited dialogue with the Egyptian authorities on poverty issues and poverty data in raw form could not, by law, be given to foreigners, the Bank's work on poverty represented an important breakthrough. With the support of the Minister of Planning, agreement was reached that an Egyptian statistician would bring the data to Washington and, working with Bank staff, produce tabulations and analyses of household survey data. It was also agreed that the final report would be a joint report of the Ministry of Planning and the World Bank. This approach led to strong ownership and transfer of analytical techniques for continuing poverty monitoring in Egypt and culminated in the Minister seeking Bank input on an action plan for poverty reduction. The process and resulting "Poverty Reduction in Egypt—Diagnosis and Strategy" (World Bank 2002c) were the most important contributions of the Bank to knowledge products in Egypt.

The Bank's knowledge of other countries is highly valued in Egypt. A 2005 retreat at Luxor on social policy, led by the Prime Minister and the World Bank president, included most of the Cabinet and brought senior officials from Mexico and Brazil, who presented their experiences of safety nets. The retreat was followed by a joint study entitled "Toward a More Effective Social Policy—Subsidies and Social Safety Net" (World Bank 2005d).

The same year the government created a Ministry of Social Solidarity. The new ministry was tasked with developing and implementing social policy reforms in this area. The Bank completed another Poverty Assessment Update in June 2007. These studies both reflected the Bank's intellectual contribution and reinforced its key position in poverty reduction and social policy discussion in Egypt.

In the private sector development and financial reforms, the Bank produced a number of significant reports that provided intellectual underpinnings and helped gain the support of government officials—a financial sector assessment program (FSAP); "Access to Finance and Economic Growth in Egypt" (World Bank 2008a); and investment climate assessments (ICAs) in 2005 and 2007. Sector analysis accompanied lending in water resources management (Integrated Water Resources Management Plan in 2005) and environment (Country Environmental Analysis in 2005). The social sectors also received considerable attention, with major reports on gender, health, and education between 1998 and 2003.

The Bank has used analytic work as a mechanism to enable it to play a wide-ranging role as policy adviser to the government and the donor community. In the energy sector, the Bank quickly delivered a series of operational policy notes, in addition to a substantive report on the economic costs of natural gas in Egypt (Nassar 2003), and has been working on energy issues with all the core ministries, including the Ministry of Finance. An energy-pricing strategy is being developed.

In infrastructure, the Bank produced a series of reports covering all aspects, including an urban transport strategy and a restructuring of railways. Following the Bank's positive and rapid response to the government's request for support for airport development (see chapter 4), the Bank became an important adviser to the Cabinet on infrastructure policy. The Bank has also provided a series of notes on telecommunications regulation, postal services, and information technology development.

A noteworthy aspect of Bank analytical and advisory services for Egypt has been the government's recent agreement to reimbursable TA from the Bank. These studies cover pension reform, regulatory reform, governance and investment support, and a wide range of supports to the telecommunications sector. Egypt is one of four countries that have benefited from both financial advisory services by the Treasury Department of the Bank and reimbursable TA by the Middle East and North Africa Regional office.

The Quality Assurance Group reviewed 12 of 23 analytical and advisory assistance (AAA) tasks completed in the fiscal 2001–03 period. Two tasks were rated highly satisfactory, nine were rated satisfactory, and one was rated marginally satisfactory. In addition, internal quality, strategic relevance, and likely impact of the tasks were rated satisfactory overall. The dialogue and dissemination efforts also were rated satisfactory.

IEG concurs with the positive assessment of recent AAA. Egyptian officials, academics, and think tanks (the Economic Research Forum and the Egypt Center for Economic Studies) generally assess the quality of Bank analytical work as high and consider that the Bank is making a major contribution to Egypt's knowledge development, particularly the Bank's reports on poverty analysis.

On balance and despite the thinness of the analytical work in the early part of the CAE period, when the Bank was still struggling with Egypt's transition from an IDA to a middle-income country, the Bank's analytical work was important in creating a knowledge base both in the Bank, to inform Bank lending, and among officials in the core ministries, particularly in poverty analysis, finance, and infrastructure. The Bank's analytic work has already started to shape Egypt's policies in these sectors.

The one area where the Bank's AAA program should have done more is the analysis of macroeconomic issues in a country economic memorandum or a development policy review. The last macro report of this kind, "Social and Structural Review" (World Bank 2001b), was prepared in 2001. This was important not only for following the macroeconomic developments in the country, but also for providing inputs to the CAS preparation and adjustment lending in the financial sector. A Development Policy Review is under preparation, to be completed in fiscal 2008.

Overview of Partnerships

Unlike in most sizeable developing countries where the Bank has had large programs, the Bank's financial support in Egypt has been lower than that of a number of other donors. USAID has long had a dominant, though declining, role, and the EU has steadily increased its assistance. The African Development Bank (AfDB), other bilateral donors, the IMF, and the United Nations Development Programme (UNDP) all have significant roles in Egypt. As a result, the Bank has been particularly aware of other donors' activities and has lent urgency to donor collaboration.

USAID has been the biggest single donor operating in Egypt, disbursing more than $5.7 billion in grants between 1999 and 2005. Nevertheless, as agreed with the Egyptian government, new commitments fell from $800 million per year in 1999 to about $400 million by 2006, with further declines possible in the near future. USAID assistance has concentrated on (i) economic growth, with an emphasis on privatization; (ii) human resource development; (iii) science and technology—a new initiative to strengthen information technology capacities; and (iv) environmental protection. Where USAID programs overlap those of the Bank, the two agencies coordinated their efforts. USAID staff in Cairo told the IEG mission that they considered Bank analytic work to be of uniformly high quality.

The EU (European Investment Bank together with the European Commission) has now become the largest source of official flows to Egypt. The European Investment Bank is providing large amounts of nonconcessional lending, and the European Commission aid program, entirely in grants, has risen steadily and may soon rival USAID. The European Commission 2007–13 program in Egypt has shifted away from TA projects toward direct funding of the Egyptian government's budget. The emphasis is on competitiveness and productivity, followed by education and health and then democracy and human rights.

The AfDB also provides substantial resources to Egypt. The AfDB has been lending to infrastructure, mostly in the power sector, but also in the agriculture, education, health, industry, and financial sectors. For example, it provided $500 million in cofinancing for the Bank's financial sector operation, tying disbursement to Bank conditionality.

The IMF had no formal program relationship in Egypt over this period, but the FSAP is a joint IMF–Bank program. IMF TA to Egypt has increased since mid-2004, including on tax and customs reform, budget classification, treasury management, monetary policy, bank restructuring, and statistics. The Bank sought IMF's views on the macroeconomic framework and short-term outlook through an assessment letter at the time of its financial sector DPL.

Other donors interviewed by the IEG mission held positive views of the quality of Bank work in Egypt and the Bank's willingness to collaborate. Where other donors had cofinancing or parallel financing arrangements with Bank lending, they considered the Bank to be an effective partner.

Praise for the quality of Bank economic and sector work was universal, with the Bank's poverty assessments being prominently mentioned as high-quality products. Some donors, however, suggested that the Bank be more proactive in alerting the donor community to new Bank studies as soon as they are published. The lack of macroeconomic reports by the Bank in recent years was seen by some as leading to over-reliance on macroeconomic analyses prepared by the IMF.

There is a formal coordination mechanism for donors operating in Egypt—the Donor Assistance Group, operating since 2001. The UNDP acts as the secretariat for the group. It has 31 members, including 21 bilateral donors and 10 multilateral organizations, representing all official donors to the country. Although it is primarily a donor forum, special guests from the Egyptian government, the private sector, and civil society organizations can be invited as appropriate. Comments from donors indicate that the Bank participated regularly and effectively in the Donor Assistance Group and in subgroups dealing with specific sectors where the Bank was active.

Chapter 3

Both exports and imports grew by 20–30 percent per year in dollar terms during the review period.
Photo by Ray Witlin, courtesy of the World Bank Photo Library.

Promoting Higher, More Sustainable Growth through Structural Reforms

Analysis suggests that Egypt could grow much faster if the unfinished structural reforms were completed, and most of the poverty and other social problems might be eased with higher growth (World Bank 1997a, 2001a, 2001b). These structural reforms were the focus of the first pillar of Bank assistance during the period under review. The pillar consisted of achieving macroeconomic stability and improving public sector governance (PSG); trade policy reforms with a competitive exchange rate; eliminating the constraints to private sector development through a better business environment; and financial sector restructuring and modernization.

Bank lending in support of the first pillar included a DPL to the financial sector (2006) and a project loan to housing finance (2006 Mortgage Finance Project), as well as nonlending services and policy dialogue.

Maintaining Macroeconomic Stability and Improving PSG

Maintaining macroeconomic stability

Background

Just prior to the beginning of the period under review, economic growth in Egypt had been strong, probably in response to a program of macroeconomic stabilization between 1991 and 1996. Nonetheless, growth during the 1990s was driven by strong demand for locally produced goods and services, in particular, nontradable and import substitutes. The contribution of the external sector was small and its share in GDP falling; exports of goods and services, for example, declined from 28 percent of GDP in 1991 to 18 percent in 1997. By 1998, fiscal deficits were increasing again, and a series of external factors (September 11, the Iraq war, a decline in Organisation for Economic Co-operation and Development growth) contributed to an eventual slowdown in growth, which fell to an average of 3 percent in the early 2000s. Inflation rose from single digits in the late 1990s to higher than 11 percent in 2004.

The Bank's objectives and program

Throughout the CAE period, the Bank's strategy gave priority to maintaining macroeconomic stability. The basic objective has been to reduce fiscal deficits and ensure that the debt burden remains sustainable. The CASs set a number of benchmarks, including a single-digit inflation rate and adopting a contribution-based pension system in the 1997 CAS; consolidating current and investment budgets, abolishing tax incentives and completing tax reform, and reducing fiscal deficits as a percentage of GDP in the 2001 CAS; and increasing the primary budget surplus and reducing the cost of subsidies as a percentage of GDP, and increasing the average maturity of domestic debt in the 2005 CAS. Each CAS determined a set of relevant indicators to evaluate the achievements of Bank objectives. The last CAS has more specific and quantitative indicators (see tables 3.1 and 3.2).

During the CAE period, the Bank's main instruments for pursuing its objectives were policy dialogue and economic and sector work. Just before the CAE period, the 1997 country economic memorandum focused on the need to increase public savings through lower fiscal deficits (higher surpluses) and reform of the social security and insurance systems. The goal was to generate higher savings and minimize contingent liabilities. Because this report was written at a time of decreasing fiscal deficits, the emphasis was on further reduction of public debt and the need for maintaining the resource inflows generated by the reform program. The 2001 social and structural review, the last macroeconomic integrative report produced by the Bank, focused more on the structure of public expenditures and revenues. However, it also cautioned about the unsustainability of fiscal deficits and focused on budget processes, recommending a more transparent budget with a longer-term framework and an expenditure system that could track and control the expenditures.

In January 2002 the government, calling attention to the impact of the September 11, 2001, events on the Egyptian economy, formally requested a $500 million policy-based loan. Over the next two years this led to a high level of dialogue that touched all major aspects of development policy.

Table 3.1: Maintaining Macroeconomic Stability – Outcome Indicators

Objective/Indicator	Baseline 1999	Outcome 2005	Comments
1. Single-digit inflation	3.7	8.8	Average inflation has been contained within single digits.
2. Improved monetary policy		Yes	Monetary policy committee has become operational.
3. Floating exchange rate	No	Yes	Floating exchange rate was introduced in 2004.
4. Reduce budget deficit (% of GNP)	(2001)	(2006)	Fiscal imbalances narrowed, as there was significant underlying adjustment in 2005–07. Further fiscal adjustment is needed.
Tax revenues	20.7	24.2	
Budget balance	–10.2	–7.5	
Primary balance	–4.4	–0.9	
5. Reduce public sector debt (% of GDP)	52.1 (1999)	72.6 (2007)	Rose to higher than 80 percent in 2004. It has been declining since then.
6. Extend average maturity of domestic debt	3 months (2004)	2.1 years (2006)	Debt management has improved.

Sources: Central Bank, IMF, and CAE mission.
Note: GDP = gross domestic product; GNP = gross national product.

Table 3.2: Egypt: Macroeconomic Indicators, 1999–2007

	1999	2000	2001	2002	2003	2004	2005	2006	2007[a]
GDP growth (annual %)[b]	6.1	5.4	3.5	3.2	3.2	4.1	4.5	6.8	7.0
Agriculture (annual % growth)	3.5	3.4	3.7	3.6	4.9	1.4	3.3	4.9	4.8
Industry (annual % growth)	6.8	5.5	3.2	3.7	5.8	3.4	5.2	5.6	7.0
Services (annual % growth)	5.1	6.9	3.5	2.8	0.5	5.9	5.6	7.5	7.5
Gross fixed capital formation (% of GDP)	20.8	18.9	17.7	17.8	16.3	16.4	17.9	18.7	22.2
Exports of goods as % of GDP[c]	5.3	7.0	8.2	8.7	10.8	14.1	16.4	18.3	19.3
Nonfuel exports as % of GDP[c]	4.1	4.5	5.1	5.8	6.6	8.7	9.9	7.9	9.9
Imports of goods as % of GDP[c]	20.4	19.5	19.0	17.9	19.5	24.7	28.7	30.1	32.3
Current account balance (% of GDP)[b]	–1.9	–1.2	0.0	0.7	2.4	4.3	3.2	0.8	1.4
External debt (% of GNI)	33.8	28.9	29.8	33.8	37.8	37.9	32.2	28.8.	24.2
Government domestic debt (% of GDP)[c]	52.1	52.1	58.6	62.4	64.6	82.4	80.5	79.8	72.6
Inflation, consumer prices (annual %)[b]	3.7	2.8	2.4	2.4	3.2	8.1	8.8	4.2	10.9

Source: World Development Indicators, except where noted.
Note: GDP = gross domestic product; GNI = gross national income.
a. 2007 figures are preliminary.
b. IMF World Economic Outlook.
c. Estimation based on Central Bank data.

A draft initiating memorandum and letter of development policy prepared in fiscal 2003 described the most important aim of Egypt's reform strategy—the creation of macroeconomic stability to achieve sustainable economic growth and social development. Management of the floating exchange rate; setting of money supply and inflation targets; and revenue enhancement and expenditure control measures to reduce the budget deficit, including the impact of tariff reform, were among the issues highlighted in the draft documents. However, the government worried about the risk of economic and political shocks that those reforms could cause in the short run. In the end, Egypt chose not to proceed with the loan.

The final area of focus was pension system reform, where the Bank worked closely with a steering committee from the Ministry of Finance to prepare a reform policy note, initially as a form of nonlending TA. In the second phase of the reform, the government paid for Bank TA (reimbursable) to provide input for a new pension system framework; a new pension law was submitted to Parliament in 2007. Under this framework, members of the existing pension systems will continue to receive their defined pensions, but the system will be closed to new entrants, who will instead have defined contributions and variable benefits. This mandatory pension system will be complemented by a voluntary system. The new system will also regulate private pension schemes.

In developing this new pension system, the Bank and Ministry of Finance officials worked closely with labor unions, the governing party, and the Labor Committee of the Parliament to come up with an acceptable program. If this plan is accepted, it will completely change the pension system and eliminate the potential liabilities of the existing system.

Outcomes

Economic activity weakened between 2000 and 2003, with GDP growth averaging only around 3 percent per year, and both private and public investment decreased as a percent of GDP. The economic slowdown was accentuated by a shortage of foreign currency, expansionary monetary and fiscal policies, and a depressed regional and global environment. Fiscal deficits increased, leading to concerns about fiscal and debt sustainability. There were policy reversals in the fiscal stance, the trade regime, and exchange rate management, and few new policy actions were undertaken on the broad reform agenda envisaged by the Bank.

The period after 2004 was completely different. A new Cabinet, led by Prime Minister Ahmed Nazif, announced bold, wide-ranging structural reforms very much in line with the reform package discussed with the Bank in the context of the policy-based loan that never materialized. Egypt made the transition to a unified, flexible exchange rate, adjusted energy prices, and tightened monetary and fiscal policy. The government started to implement fiscal reforms in 2005.

On the revenue side, corporate and personal income tax rates were reduced, and the tax base widened. Tax exemptions were mostly eliminated. On the expenditure side, a single treasury account was introduced, together with tightening controls on public expenditures. A primary dealer system was introduced to improve domestic debt management and reduce over time its cost to the budget. The privatization program was reactivated. This fiscal program was aimed at bringing the fiscal deficit down by at least 1 percent of GDP annually for five years between 2005 and 2010.

As a result of these reforms and supportive macroeconomic policies, economic activity began to accelerate after 2004. Inflation fell sharply in 2005, and real interest rates turned positive. Growth acceleration was relatively broad based, with services and industry growing more strongly. The economy grew at about 7 percent per annum in 2006 and 2007. On the demand side, there was a sharp increase in private investment, accompanied by some growth in consumption. Public investment continued to decline. Inflation has been contained within single digits, except for fluctuations in 2006 and early 2007. Nevertheless, inflationary pressures from strong domestic demand and rising world food prices persist and are at risk of accelerating.

The fiscal deficit declined from 10.2 percent of GDP in 2002 to 7.5 percent in 2007. Primary deficits, according to the new budgetary accounts' classification, also declined from 4.4 percent to 0.9 percent over the same period. The average maturity of domestic debt was lengthened to 2.1 years by December 2006. The debt-to-GDP ratio decreased from 82 percent in 2004 to 73 percent in 2007. Revenue gains from the sale of public enterprises are being used partly to pay down the debt, partly to cover the contingent liabilities of the public banks and state-owned enterprises, and partly to meet the needs of lower-income households and underprivileged areas.

Subsidies have been one of the reasons for large fiscal deficits. The two main components have been subsidies on food and energy. Although food subsidies have been steady at around 1–2 percent of GDP, recent international oil price increases led to rising energy subsidies. Domestic price adjustments for fuel and electricity in 2004 and 2006 could not keep pace with the international price increases; therefore, energy subsidies increased to almost 7 percent of GDP in 2005–06. After further price adjustments in 2007, energy subsidies gradually declined to 5.5 percent of GDP in 2006–07, although they are still large and fiscally costly.[1]

Despite the significant structural reforms in the recent period and positive economic developments, output growth and macroeconomic balances remain fragile in Egypt. Fiscal deficits and government debt level remain high. Under the current pattern of funding the budget deficit, public borrowing from the domestic banking system eats up domestic credit and crowds out the private sector, undermining its participation in economic activity. Therefore, further progress in reducing budgetary expenditures, including the subsidies and in increasing public revenues, is needed to maintain macroeconomic stability in the face of the current turbulence in global financial markets.

Egypt is less exposed to shifts in global economic conditions than it was in the early 2000s. The establishment of a well-functioning foreign exchange market, the prevalence of a current account surplus, lower external debt, increased foreign exchange reserves, and strengthened policy frameworks have all helped make the economy more resilient to external shocks. But although the Egyptian economy has become more resilient, it would still be affected in a potentially serious way by a pronounced global slowdown, rising world food prices, and deteriorating terms of trade.

Assessing the Bank's contribution

Bank studies and draft policy loan documents in this reform area were prepared in the first half of the CAE period; no major macroeconomic report has been produced since fiscal 2001. Nevertheless, the Bank's analysis and advice on the conduct of macroeconomic policy were sound and consistent and remained valid throughout the period. Despite the IMF's role, the Bank should have had its own assessment of macroeconomic developments, which would have helped both the Bank and the government to better prioritize the reform program and the Bank's role in it. In recent years, the Bank has made a significant contribution in pension reform, which serves as a good example of reimbursable TA to a middle-income country.

Improving PSG

Background

Egypt had significant PSG issues at the beginning of the CAE period. According to the World Bank Institute, although the country had scores similar to the 1998 Middle East and North Africa average in regulatory quality, rule of law, and control of corruption, its scores were below average in voice and accountability, political stability, and government effectiveness. Tax collection involved arbitrary and unpredictable treatment of tax payers, and the tax code had incentives that distorted resource allocation. The government budget was affected by off-budget entities, used a manual accounting system, had fragmented budget preparation processes, and lacked an internal audit function. The Central Audit Agency and Parliamentary Budget Committee did not exercise their functions as external auditors.

The civil service was underpaid, lacked a merit-based system, and had weak capacity throughout. The number of public sector employees (5.2 million in 1999, excluding police and the military) was high by regional and international standards. The country was an "extreme" case of centralized government. All governorate, district, and municipal budgets were part of the central budget. Transfers of funds from the central government accounted for 90 percent of local revenues. Most public services were delivered by central ministries operating through their own (decentralized) local staff. Although the country had several agencies that combated corruption, most lacked independence.

The Bank's objectives and program

The 2001 CAS discussed PSG issues for the first time in the history of Bank assistance to Egypt. The CAS objectives included only one governance area, where there was clear government ownership: tax policy and administration reform. This involved not only tax policy and administration reform but also setting up monitorable standards in major revenue-collection functions and abolishing most tax incentives.

There were also Bank AAA activities in public financial management (PFM). These activities aimed to improve the transparency of the budget process, accounting, and public procurement and audit, which thus can be considered implicit but not explicit objectives of the 2001 CAS. In the 2005 CAS, objectives in the tax area continued, and the other governance activities broadened to include public service delivery through sectoral projects in education, health, and energy.

Bank support for PSG has been through AAA. The Bank delivered a set of joint government-Bank task force reports in 1999 addressing the civil service and tax policy and administration.

The Bank continued pointing out these areas as major weaknesses in PSG in subsequent core reports. A report on the ICA (World Bank 2005e) showed taxation as a major impediment to doing business. The Bank's role in tax reform has diminished since mid-2004, as the new government requested the IMF to take the lead in this area.

The Bank delivered extensive analytical work in PFM, which has proved useful to the current government. Early in the period, between 2001 and 2004, the Bank supported the first steps of developing a performance-based budgeting system. The Country Financial Accountability Assessment and the Country Procurement Assessment Report, both delivered in fiscal 2004, focused on the central government's PFM and procurement systems. Major recommendations included implementing modern internal audits, implementing a Treasury Single Account (TSA), introducing a government financial management information system, and reforming the public procurement system. Because the government did not agree to a full public expenditure review (PER), the Bank produced instead nine public expenditure policy notes, covering six sectors, and three fiscal and budget notes.[2] The Bank completed in 2006 an Institutional Financial Management Capacity Assessment for education, health, transport, and water, which included a government-wide assessment of the PFM system.

The Bank carried out an assessment of the investment climate in 2005 and an update in 2007, which helped the government initiate comprehensive reforms in tax policy, business deregulation, and anticorruption. Following these assessments, the government requested support for anticorruption efforts from the Bank through the World Bank Institute and reimbursable TA. These represent the first steps in the anticorruption agenda in Egypt. The Institute co-managed the first high-level dialogue on corruption in Egypt in 2006 and is developing an anticorruption curriculum and training of trainers for the Ministry of Investment and the Ministry of Administrative Reform. The World Bank Institute also took a lead role in a workshop for the establishment of a single financial supervisory agency. Through the fiscal 2007 regulatory reform and governance assistance and reimbursable TA project, the Bank delivered a manual for a state-owned assets and investment management program (privatization) and a draft Freedom of Information Act, which includes a comparative analysis of similar laws in other countries. Support for the Ministry of Investment to review the regulatory framework has been under way. The FSAP and the financial sector DPL, by addressing the regulatory framework of that sector, are supporting the anticorruption agenda.

Outcomes

The most important progress on PSG during the CAE period has been in the tax area, which was the only area with an explicit objective in the CAS. A month after taking office in 2004, the new cabinet initiated the drafting of an income tax law to align Egypt with international practice. The new law eliminated exemptions and new tax holidays (about 3,000 in all); cut tax rates (a flat profit tax of 20 percent and maximum personal income tax from 32 to 20 percent); clarified rules and replaced universal assessments with self-assessments and sample audits; and reduced the scope for interpreting the amount of tax owed. These measures have reduced opportunities for administrative corruption. A large taxpayer unit was established in 2005, and the sales and income tax departments were merged in 2006.

Budget revenues increased from 20.7 percent of GDP in 2002 to 24.2 percent in 2006–07, mainly with the positive impacts of income tax reform and strong growth. There was a slight decline in trade tax revenues caused by tariff reduction (see table 3.3). Budget expenditures declined slightly as a result of restraints on wages and public investments. Budget and primary deficits have declined, but they are still high for macroeconomic stability. Fiscal consolidation has remained a priority. This requires additional fiscal measures and a further reduction of fuel subsidies.

In PFM, progress was mixed. The budget document was made public for the first time in

Table 3.3: Budget Details (percentage of GDP)

	Fiscal 2002	Fiscal 2004	Fiscal 2007
Revenue	20.7	21.0	24.2
Taxes	13.7	13.8	15.5
Income and property	5.5	6.1	6.8
Trade	1.9	1.4	1.4
Expenditures	30.5	30.1	29.8
Wages and salaries	8.1	7.7	7.0
Interest	5.7	6.3	6.5
Capital expenditure	5.2	4.7	3.3
Budget balance	−10.2	−9.5	−7.5
Primary balance	−4.4	−3.1	−0.9

Source: IMF; budget sector fiscal 2007 data are preliminary.
Note: The fiscal year begins on July 1. Budget data are consistent with the Government Finance Statistics 2001 classification.

fiscal 2004–05, and it became more comprehensive. The 2005–06 budget covered quasifiscal activities for payments to state-owned enterprises and consumers and is compliant with the IMF's chart of accounts; and the government subscribed to the IMF's Special Data Dissemination Standard.[3] The TSA was introduced in November 2006, replacing some 5,000 accounts (48,000 subaccounts) that to a great extent had allowed spending at the holder's discretion. The TSA improved the Ministry of Finance's cash management and control. A new procurement law allowed the incorporation of price escalation/adjustment mechanisms in government contracts, set a maximum period for the government to pay eligible invoices, and helped centralize purchases. These measures are currently being implemented. The procurement agency (the General Authority for Government Services) has centralized the purchasing of selected items for a number of ministries. According to the agency, the price for some of these items has decreased by as much as 20 percent in 2006. Staff from the procurement agency acknowledged the Bank's support.

Most of the main PFM problems remain, however. The Ministry of Finance still lacks modern internal audit units. External auditing has improved only marginally. Although constitutional amendments in 2007 increased Parliament's role in oversight of the budget, its technical capacity is limited. The Central Audit Agency remains a weak external auditor. The budget preparation remains fragmented, with the Ministry of Finance and Ministry of Planning separately deciding current and investment budgets. Programmatic budgeting has been piloted in a few ministries, but overall progress has slowed, especially since 2004, despite the government's broader reform orientation.

A broad range of indicators of corruption show that it is still a serious problem in Egypt, and perceptions have not yet improved. Nonetheless, in some specific areas there are signs of progress. The government has launched reforms that have reduced direct interaction with the bureaucracy and reduced its discretion capabilities.[4] Tax simplification (for example, clear guidelines, risk-based auditing, and introduction of hotlines) and the launch of e-government services are two examples. The Ministry of Investment and the General Authority for Investment and Free Zones have led efforts to reduce business regulations.

Improvements introduced by these indirect measures have been substantial. The proportion of manufacturing firms reporting informal payments to officials fell from 27 percent in 2004 to 16 percent in 2006. The proportion of inspections where informal payments were expected also declined. The government signed the United Nations convention against corruption in 2003, and the Prime Minister established a committee in the Ministry of State for Administration Development to combat corruption. During the last two years the governing party has led an anticorruption campaign that has resulted in convictions of some prominent figures, including a former minister and a former governor.

Assessing the Bank's Contribution

Although many factors influence reforms in a complex country like Egypt, experience shows that the Bank's AAA on PSG issues can encourage progress in selected areas, even in the absence of lending. Bank support contributed to recent reforms in two ways. First, it provided evidence for champions in government to push comprehensive reforms. The early analytical work on tax reform and the ICA diagnosis prompted officials to implement comprehensive tax policy and administrative reforms, although the IMF provided more prominent guidance on the details during the implementation phase. By highlighting corruption as one of the main barriers for business, the ICA also led the government to request additional support from the Bank and to take the first steps in the anticorruption agenda.

Second, Bank studies provided the analytical basis for the recent reforms in PFM, procurement, and the financial sector. The government relied heavily on the Bank's inputs in introducing the TSA and reforming public procurement. Other donors' country programs—USAID in particular—have benefited as well from the Report on the Observance of Standards and Codes: Accounting and Auditing and the FSAP.

The question of whether more Bank pressure on the governance issues could have achieved greater progress is an exceedingly difficult one to answer. The government was clear in saying that it would not tolerate unwelcome pressure in the context of the 2001 CAS. In the end, the government did take steps forward, and there is little evidence that it would have taken more as a result of further overt action on the Bank's part, particularly given the inherently political underpinnings of the support from some of the major development partners. In line with one of the key findings of IEG's public sector reform evaluation (IEG 2008b), the indirect strategy appears to have been reasonably relevant and effective under the specific circumstances.

Trade Reform

Background

Egypt had a very restrictive trade regime throughout the 1990s and early 2000s, with multiple tariff rates (27 at one point), ad hoc surcharges and controls on imports, and other administrative barriers for exports. The regulatory regime, including customs and the physical infrastructure for trade, was inadequate. The trade regime had a strong anti-export bias and, coupled with a noncompetitive exchange rate during most of the 1990s, created significant barriers to trade with the rest of the world. Manufacturing exports grew more slowly than world trade growth or domestic output. Especially during the late 1990s, the share of nonfuel exports to GDP declined to less than 5 percent.

The Bank's objectives and program

Bank strategy has been to help create a dynamic nonfuel export sector and to help the Egyptian economy be more competitive and better integrated into the world economy by reducing trade tariffs and eliminating customs surcharges. Both the 1997 and 2001 CASs aimed at a non-oil export growth of 10 percent per annum. The 2001 CAS targeted reducing maximum tariffs, from 40 percent to 30 percent, and eliminating the customs surcharge. The 2005 CAS aimed at reducing the number of days to clear imported goods by improving customs administration. Most Bank program objectives at this subpillar were precise and quantitative (see table 3.4).

Prior to the period under review, the Bank had carried out a detailed analysis of the ports, customs, and duty drawback systems, along with restrictive quality control and other administrative barriers. The 2001 social and structural review also identified factors constraining export growth, as well as overall economic growth, including the appreciating exchange rate and the investment environment. Two additional fiscal 2001 reports assessed constraints to exports: an agriculture export strategy and an Export Promotion Task Force report.

Lending support was modest. Only one TA project, the Port Sector Reform Learning and Innovation Loan, was approved in fiscal 1998, just before the beginning of the period under review. A planned export development project for fiscal 2000 and an agricultural exports project in fiscal 2004 were never approved, nor was a structural adjustment operation, where trade reform was a major component.

Outcomes

Starting in 2004, trade policy underwent profound reforms, far more extensive than recommended by the Bank. Exchange rate management, identified as one of the major constraints to trade expansion, has been reformed. In addition, new regulations have been put in place for industrial zones. Improvements were envisaged for 2009 in import clearance and cargo management, but with a new private port, new private sector concessions in airports and ports, and new free-trade zones, the targeted improvements appear to be on schedule.

Tariff reform was particularly notable: the number of tariff bands went down from 27 to 6; import surcharges of 3 to 4 percent were abolished; and between 1998 and 2007, the simple average tariff declined from 25 to 14 percent, the weighted average from 13.7 to 6.9 percent (table 3.4), below that of other middle-income countries. Thus, Egypt has moved from a restrictive trade regime to a more open one and in the process surpassed its multilateral commitment under the World Trade Organization.

A new customs law and implementing regulation simplified the customs regime. By 2007, customs clearance was reported to have fallen to 1 day from more than 20 days in 2003. Consequently, cargo storage time in warehouses dropped from 28 to 2 days, thereby reducing transaction costs for exports and imports. Customs disputes were observed to have fallen from 35 percent of all customs transactions to less than 1 percent.

Table 3.4: Trade Reform Outcome Indicators

	Baseline 1998	Outcome 2005–06
Tariff (simple average MFN)[a]	25.1	14.4
Applied weighted average[a]	13.7	6.9
Imports (% of GDP)	21.0	29.4
Exports (% of GDP)	5.9	17.3
Nonfuel exports (% of GDP)	4.2	9.1
Export growth (annual %)	–8.7	32.9
Nonfuel exports growth (annual %)	6.5	13.5
Current account (% of GDP)	–2.6	2.6
FDI ($ millions)	509	6,111
FDI (share of GDP)[b]	1.1	5.3

Source: IMF Direction of Trade Statistics yearbook (2006), except where indicated.

Note: FDI = foreign direct investment; GDP = gross domestic product; MFN = most favored nation.

a. World Bank WITS: Baseline 1998, outcome 2006.

b. From Central Bank monthly tables, September 2007.

Exchange rate management has also improved in recent years. In 2004 the foreign exchange regime was unified. The government eliminated controls on current account transactions in compliance with the IMF Article VIII obligation on this, set up an interbank foreign exchange market, and abolished export surrender requirements. Although the exchange rate is still "managed," it became more competitive in the early 2000s with a large devaluation. It has recently started to appreciate again, driven primarily by external inflows, but it remains more competitive than it has been since fiscal 1993.

The large correction of the nominal and real exchange rates during 2001–03 boosted competitiveness and exports. The oil boom in the Gulf region has increased workers' remittances and tourism revenues. Starting in 2001, the current account moved to surplus (from a deficit in the late 1990s). The growth rate of non-oil exports (in current U.S. dollars) over fiscal 1998 to fiscal 2006 period was 13.5 percent per annum, thus surpassing the 10 percent target of Bank strategy; the share of nonfuel exports to GDP almost doubled during the review period and reached 10 percent in 2005–06. The capital account registered record levels of foreign direct investment and strong portfolio flows. Official reserves reached the equivalent of more than six months of imports of goods and services.

Despite these impressive achievements, Egypt continues to lag behind other emerging economies, such as Hungary, Malaysia, Poland, and Turkey, in the degree of export diversification and performance. The country still exports few manufactured goods, and greater diversification of non-oil exports is needed to further stimulate its growth potential and employment generation and to reduce volatility of exports. In addition, a more diversified export structure can help stimulate new industries and expand existing industries elsewhere in the economy. Export diversification can also help bring about higher productivity through knowledge spillovers. Finally, export diversification can help reduce the volatility of export revenue by restricting dependence to a limited number of products that are subject to major price and volume fluctuations (such as agriculture and oil; World Bank 2007b).

Assessing the Bank's contribution

The Bank carried out major analyses of a wide range of trade issues both before and during the CAE period, although lending assistance in this area was modest. Although it had a continuous dialogue with the authorities on the trade regime, its analyses were used only when a reform-oriented government came to power in 2004. One Egyptian academic noted that it was impossible to think about trade issues in Egypt without reference to Bank trade work, both in Egypt and globally. The Bank's knowledge products and institutional support have thus made important contributions to successful trade reforms in Egypt.

Private Sector Development

Background

Egypt had long had restrictive policies on private investment and other business activities; the legal system, tax structure, and administration were not business friendly. Furthermore, the public sector owned a significant portion of the economy. There had been sales of public enterprises prior to the start of the review period, but the stock of state-owned enterprises was still significant at the beginning of the CAE period.

The Bank's objectives and program

The Bank has consistently focused on the regulatory environment and investment climate for private sector development. All CASs addressed this issue, with assessments of the main constraints to private sector activity and policy recommendations on improving entry and exit, reforming the tax regime, and accelerating the privatization program. In addition, increased private and foreign investment and an improvement of corporate governance were objectives of the 2005 CAS.

The Bank worked on private sector development through economic and sector work, nonlending TA, and reimbursable TA. A key undertaking was an ICA in 2005 and an update in 2007. The 2005 ICA identified as major constraints tax rates and tax administration, macroeconomic instability, regulatory policy uncertainty, illegal competition, and corruption. These were rated as "major" or "very severe" constraints by more than 50 percent of respondents. The 2007 ICA update corrected certain defects in the 2005 sample design. The government used the ICA and the update to redirect its reform program, and the update was used to measure reform achievements. A new ICA is planned for 2008.

Two additional studies were the Administrative Barriers by the Foreign Investment Advisory Service and—more important—the Bank's study of free-trade zones. The evaluation of the zones is being followed up by a more detailed study by USAID. The Foreign Investment Advisory Service has been providing assistance on institutional development and the legal framework for all commercial investment in Egypt to the General Authority for Investment and Free Zones. The Bank and IFC have been providing assistance on public-private partnerships for the development and implementation of legal and regulatory frameworks in many sectors.

Between fiscal 1997 and fiscal 2007, IFC invested in 57 projects for $842 million in new commitments, with 14 percent of the amount in equity and 86 percent in loans. The portfolio was diversified and included investments in the financial sector, power, manufacturing, ports, oil and gas, metals, agribusiness, and health care. IFC also undertook 37 advisory services operations for about $12 million. The advisory services were evenly spread across the five business lines—access to finance, business-enabling environment, environment and social sustainability, infrastructure, and value addition to firms (see appendix B for details on the IFC program in Egypt).

Outcomes

With improvements in 5 of the 10 areas covered by the *Doing Business 2008* report (World Bank 2008b), Egypt has outpaced other reformers. "Deep" reforms included reducing the minimum capital required to start a business, cutting by half the time and cost of start-up, reducing fees for registering property, and easing the bureaucracy in getting construction permits. In addition, Egypt launched new one-stop shops for traders at Egyptian ports, cutting the time to import by seven days and the time to export by five days. Egypt also established a new private credit bureau that will soon be making it easier for borrowers to get credit. Egypt's ranking in *Doing Business* has improved from 165th place in 2005 to 126th place in 2007. However, despite this impressive improvement, Egypt still lags behind most countries in the Middle East and North Africa Region.

One of the constraints to private sector growth has been the large share of the public sector in the economy. Privatization has accelerated in recent years with the sale of large companies, including Egypt Telecom, banks, and manufacturing firms. The Bank has contributed to the continuing efforts in privatization. Although the share of private sector contribution to GDP has not moved much, the share of the private sector in industrial activity, defined as nonpetroleum and mining, has increased from 79 percent in fiscal 1999 to almost 90 percent in fiscal 2007 (table 3.5).

Six kinds of special zones have been developed to mitigate administrative and infrastructural constraints faced by new investors. The most important of the six is the Qualified Industrial Zone, which allows the firms to use inputs from Israel and receive trade preferences in the U.S. market. A similar zone is planned for Turkish investors, where inputs from Turkey, which has a common market with EU, can be used to receive greater preferences from the EU market. There are also plans for special zones for different countries, such as China and Russia. Most zones do not give tax breaks or exemptions, and they are controlled by different agencies. The General Authority for Investment and Free Zones has also established a one-stop center that is expected to facilitate new investments.

Table 3.5: Private Sector Development Indicators

	Baseline 1998–99	Outcome 2006–07
Number of public companies	262	164
Private sector share in GDP	67.9	66.7
Private sector share in nonpetroleum industry	79.4	88.6
Private investment/GDP	10.5	12.2

Sources: Ministry of Investment and CAE mission.
Note: GDP = gross domestic product.

One of the most significant policy changes in the past few years for improving investment climate has been the reform of the personal income and corporate tax system, listed as a key constraint in the 2005 ICA. Personal and corporate income tax rates were modified in 2005, lowering top rates and eliminating exemptions. In addition, the stamp tax was reformed, reform of tax administration was started, and large taxpayer units were introduced. The 2007 ICA update confirmed that income taxes and administration are now seen as less of a constraint.

Assessing the Bank's contribution

ICAs have been successful in highlighting key constraints to private economic activity. They have also been used to direct and measure the results of the deregulation agenda. Other donor agencies have also been active in this area, and the Bank might have used its limited resources to focus more on financial and other constraints to private sector development. The Foreign Investment Advisory Service is also very active and will probably play an important role in helping the General Authority for Investment and Free Zones and the Ministry of Investments to rationalize investment incentives.

There was little collaboration with the IFC in the 1999–2004 period. Bank-IFC collaboration has picked up since mid-2004, underpinned by the shift in government policy to emphasize private sector development, public-private participation, and privatization. The factors that have contributed to improving the country partnership between IFC and the Bank include increasing Bank activities focused on private sector development and the financial sector; government pressure for a coordinated World Bank Group role; both a Bank and an IFC presence in Cairo, where IFC's hub in the Middle East and North Africa is located; and close working relationships between Bank and IFC staff on advisory activities through the Private Enterprise Partnership for the Middle East and North Africa Region. In an overall sense, collaboration between the Bank and IFC in Egypt is judged to be adequate over the CAE period (see appendix B; IEG 2007).

Financial Sector Reform

Background

The Egyptian financial system was identified as a core constraint to growth in all the CASs. The financial sector was dominated by four state commercial banks, with high operating costs, low interest margins, and poor portfolio quality, although the magnitude of bad loans was not fully known. The prudential regulatory system needed significant strengthening. Finally, enterprise surveys suggested that the banking system was not meeting the needs of small and medium enterprises. The insurance and mortgage sectors were underdeveloped, dominated by the public sector, and had serious problems with their legal frameworks. The capital market was similarly embryonic.

The Bank's objectives and program

The Bank's financial sector assistance strategy had three main objectives: (i) reduce the pervasive state ownership of financial institutions, (ii) strengthen the institutional structure (central bank, banking system, and supervisory authority) and regulatory framework, and (iii) increase access to resources to permit new and reformed institutions to meet the needs of their clients. The results sought were to enable the financial sector to generate long-term funds for investments, to improve banking efficiency, and to minimize contingent liabilities of the public banking system.

All three CASs established many indicators to evaluate the achievement of Bank program objectives. Among the three CASs, the 2005 CAS objectives were the most precise and quantified, such as reducing the share of public ownership from 65 percent in 2004 to 40 percent in 2009, increasing the share of private business sector credit from 54 percent in 2004 to 64 percent in 2009, and privatizing at least one of the four major banks (see table 3.6).

The Bank and IMF together carried out an FSAP in 2002. Initially, the government did not respond to those recommendations or share the results with other donors active in the financial sector. In 2004, a new Central Bank governor and the new government prepared a far-reaching, comprehensive financial sector reform program covering the banking system, insurance industry, capital markets, and mortgage finance. This ambitious financial sector reform program heavily relied on the findings of the FSAP.

In fiscal 2006, the Bank, working with other donors, supported this program with a financial sector DPL ($500 million) and an institutional reform TA program. Following the Bank's lead, USAID provided $1.2 billion in the form of budget support. The AfDB, which from the outset was assessing the potential for assistance to the government program, conducted its appraisal of the operation jointly with the Bank and provided $500 million. The total financing package reached $2.2 billion. Other donors—notably USAID, the EU, the European Central Bank, and the U.S. Federal Reserve—have provided TA in many areas of financial sector reform.

The Bank also provided nonlending TA on the mortgage finance system starting in 2000, which was used by the government to start restructuring the system.[5] This work eventually led to a project. The Mortgage Finance Project in fiscal 2007 ($37 million) enabled banks and nonbank

Table 3.6: Egypt: Selected Banking Sector Indicators

	Baseline 1998	Outcome 2005–06
Capital adequacy ratio		
Capital (net worth) to assets	5.0	5.5
Capital adequacy ratio	10.7	16.3
Size		
Central bank assets to GDP	25.5	41.6
Deposit money bank assets to GDP	74.3	79.6
Financial system deposits to GDP	66.9	90.5
M2 to GDP	72.8	92.4
Credit		
Domestic credit provided by banking sector (% of GDP)	92.6	105.5
Domestic credit to private sector (% of GDP)	52.7	52.4
Share of credit to public sector	24.2	16.6

Sources: Central Bank; CAE mission.
Note: GDP = gross domestic product.

lenders to begin offering long-term market-based mortgage loans for residential housing. The proceeds of the Bank loan will be on-lent (loaned in turn by the government) to the Egyptian Company for Mortgage Refinancing as a line of credit in Egyptian pounds at a market rate of interest. This was one of the first operations in local currency approved by the Bank in 2006. The loan became effective in 2007.

Outcomes

Significant progress has been made in financial sector reform since September 2004. Positive achievements include: (i) privatization of the fourth largest state-owned bank, the Bank of Alexandria; (ii) an audit of all state-owned banks by independent auditors; (iii) the divestiture of public sector shares in joint venture banks; (iv) restructuring of the remaining state-owned banks; (v) consolidation of the banking sector through the enforcement of stricter prudential rules, which resulted in the exit of small and weak banks and reduced the overall number of banks from 57 in 2004 to 43 in 2006; (vi) a reduction of nonperforming loans; (vii) the emergence of the Central Bank of Egypt as a modern central bank, focused on monetary policy and the regulation and supervision of banking system; and (viii) marked improvements in bank regulation and supervision.

There have also been important achievements in the nonbanking financial sector: (i) restructuring of the state-owned insurance companies; (ii) enhancement of the capacity to supervise insurance and private pensions; (iii) preparation of the legal and institutional framework for developing a well-functioning mortgage market; (iv) establishment of credit bureaus; and (v) strengthening of the government debt market.

Most banking indicators have shown steady improvements in the CAE period (see table 3.6). The privatization of one major public bank (Bank of Alexandria) and the divestiture of state shares in joint venture banks reduced the share of public ownership in banking from 65 percent in 2004 to 47 percent in March 2008. As a result, the private sector now owns the majority of banking assets. The banks are, on average, stronger and the financial sector deeper. One measure of depth, M2/GDP, showed a healthy increase, from 73 percent in 1998 to 92 percent in 2006. Overall credit by the banking sector also expanded over this period. Banks' holdings of government securities rose from 23 percent of GDP in 2002 to 35 percent in 2006. Credit to the public sector declined as a share of total credit, but credit to the private sector has been stagnant as a percent of GDP in recent years, as banks started tightening lending procedures and controls in response to regulatory reforms.

This is typical development in a period of large-scale restructuring and privatization. There was also significant progress in developing capital markets, especially the equity market. The corporate sector has become more resilient with the recovery of economic activity, but access to long-term finance still seems restricted. Since the 2002 FSAP, the average debt-equity ratio of the largest listed firms has declined from 66 to 48 percent, a very low ratio by international standards (the average ratio for 52 developed and emerging countries was 75 percent in the same period).

In spite of substantial progress, however, financial sector reforms remain incomplete. Completing them will require an initial focus on finalizing bank reforms, but efforts to develop the nonbanking parts of the sector and diversify the financial system also need to continue. This is important to ensure a more balanced financial sector that is capable of performing all the intermediation functions and diversifying risks.

As in many other developing countries, lack of access to finance is considered a major constraint to firms' growth in Egypt, with around 26 percent of 2006 ICA respondents citing it as an obstacle. Financial and operational restructuring of the remaining commercial and specialized state banks should be completed, including the privatization of another large public bank (Banque du Caire) in the near future. The 2007 FSAP update is providing a menu of options for additional financial sector reforms.

Assessing the Bank's contribution

During the CAE period, the Bank worked closely with the government on financial sector reform and supported it with financial resources. More importantly, through analytical work, the Bank supported almost all facets of the program. The policy dialogue was continuous. The financial sector DPL was closely supervised from the field by the task team leader, in addition to periodic supervision missions occurring. The Bank team was strengthened by banking restructuring experts from the Region and the anchor, who helped the government design the restructuring plans for the state-owned banks and provided substantive comments and input in drafting related laws and regulations.

In addition, the Bank has been the coordinator of the TA supplied by the donors, which is a critical component of the program. The Bank's contribution to financial sector reform is considered significant.

Summary

Egypt's GDP growth decelerated between 2000 and 2003 compared with the late 1990s, averaging only around 3.2 percent per annum. The loss of growth momentum was accompanied by a decrease in both private and public investment, as well as macroeconomic instability. Fiscal deficits were rising, leading to concerns about fiscal and debt sustainability.

Once the government embarked on its program of macroeconomic reforms in mid-2004, fiscal balances improved, the ratio of debt to GDP decreased, and inflation came down. The tax system underwent a significant improvement, and the pension system is being revamped, although this process is not yet complete. Nevertheless, government subsidies remain high: food subsidies have been contained, but energy subsidies have not. Mainly because of the surge in international oil prices, energy subsidies still amounted to almost 5.5 percent of GDP in 2006–07, a level that is clearly not consistent with continued fiscal discipline. On PSG, budgetary transparency, revenue administration, and public procurement improved, but these are only a limited part of the whole picture, which remains problematic.

Thus, it is no surprise that the overall governance indicators for Egypt have not improved. Therefore, for this first subcomponent—maintaining macroeconomic stability and improving PSG—the rating for the outcome of Bank assistance has been assessed as moderately satisfactory.

In trade reform, major progress was made after 2004. The trade regime was liberalized and simplified, and protection was significantly reduced. The foreign exchange regime was also reformed and the exchange rate is both more competitive and flexible. These reforms have had a dramatic impact on exports and foreign direct investment inflows. The outcome of this aspect of Bank assistance is considered moderately satisfactory.

Table 3.7: Pillar 1: Summary Outcome Rating

Objective	Outcomes
Promoting higher, more sustainable growth through structural reforms	**Moderately satisfactory**
Maintaining macroeconomic stability and improving PSG	Moderately satisfactory
Trade reform	Moderately satisfactory
Private sector development	Satisfactory
Financial sector reform	Satisfactory

Source: IEG.
Note: PSG = public sector governance.

The Bank's objectives for private sector development were largely met, for deregulation, investment promotion, and privatization and outcomes are considered satisfactory.

Financial sector reform is a long-term process, but this too has shown significant progress, with outcome indicators generally showing satisfactory improvement. IEG considers this aspect of the Bank's assistance to have a satisfactory outcome.

Based on these results, reflected in the rating of each subpillar, the first pillar of Bank assistance—promoting higher, more sustainable growth through structural reforms—is rated as *moderately satisfactory* (see table 3.7).

Chapter 4

Planning for operations seeks to help the Egyptian government enhance services such as energy provision and transportation in a sustainable manner. Photo by Ray Witlin, courtesy of the World Bank Photo Library.

Improving Water Resources Management, Infrastructure, and Environment

The Bank's CASs have always devoted considerable efforts to help the government of Egypt in rural areas focus on water resources management, rural finance, and rural development projects. The Bank's main instrument during the review period has been specific investment projects. Analytical work—especially economic and sector work—has increased, particularly from 2004, including reimbursable TA.

The Bank had several objectives in infrastructure: help the government increase the involvement of the private sector in public infrastructure investments, help improve the policy and regulatory framework, and provide direct financing support for public investment in power generation and transportation (ports, roads, railways, and urban transportation). In environment, the Bank's objectives were preserving Egypt's natural—particularly marine—resources, reducing urban and industrial pollution to improve water and air quality, and monitoring and enforcing the environmental protection laws and regulations.

Water Resources Management, Agriculture, and Rural Development

Background

Egypt's water requirements are increasing as a result of population growth, rising living standards, and the need to foster industrialization and reclaim new lands. Egypt is an arid country with limited rainfall. Freshwater resources are limited to the Nile River and, to a much lesser extent, the groundwater sources in the deserts and Sinai. Egypt shares the Nile with nine other countries.

Much of the difference between Egypt's annual 55.5 billion cubic meter (m^3) water allotment and its current 68.3 billion m^3 use comes from water reuse. On its way from the Aswan High Dam to the sea, Nile water is used over and over again to irrigate crops in the valley and delta. Water is becoming increasingly scarce when measured by a simple indicator such as per capita renewable water supply, which went down from 910 m^3 per year in the late 1990s to 778 m^3 recently (FAO 2005)—among the lowest in the world.

The limiting factor for Egyptian agriculture, which still generates more than one-third of total employment, is water. Most of Egypt's water resources (about 80 percent) are used for agricultural production. Virtually all Egyptian agriculture lands are irrigated. Although the share of agriculture in GDP fell steadily from greater than 20 percent in the mid-1980s to 17 percent in 1999, this sector was important for economic growth and rural incomes at the beginning of the CAE review period.

The Bank's objectives and program

The Bank supported most of the goals expressed in the government's 20-year vision and 5-year development plans: ensure sustainable natural resources management, raise agricultural incomes, and reduce income disparities across regions. Where it differed was on the expansion of agricultural land areas ("frontier development"), a recurring government objective involving reclamation of new land from the desert. The Bank's objectives in the three CASs (1997, 2001, and 2005) can be summarized as follows:

- Improve the management of water and land resources, including the institutional arrangements for water resources management.
- Improve agricultural productivity by increasing the efficiency of water usage.
- Improve the cost recovery of water infrastructure investments, including operation and maintenance.
- Reduce rural poverty and interregional disparities.

Although the CASs specified indicators for monitoring the results, many were not easily monitorable or precise in the timeframe of the CASs.

The Bank has had a long involvement in rural development, water management, and agriculture in Egypt, with programs stretching over 25 years. The Bank's portfolio in these sectors consisted of 13 project loans: seven projects in water resources management, three in agriculture, and three in rural development. These loans amounted to roughly $1.2 billion, or 39 percent of total commitments of ongoing and new lending operations in Egypt ($3.1 billion) during the review period. The bulk of the funds were for water resources management, that is, drainage, irrigation, and pumping stations (see table 4.1). The Bank's lending for rural development was limited: it consisted of three small projects, only some 5 percent of lending within the themes of water resources management, agriculture, and rural development.

Water resources management

Egypt faced a major challenge in developing and maintaining a large water infrastructure. The Bank has provided significant financial resources, TA, and leadership for the improvement of vast areas of Egypt's cultivated lands. The objectives of the Bank's involvement in this sector have been to safeguard—and where possible increase—agricultural productivity as well as the incomes of small farmers by improving irrigation and drainage conditions; reclaiming the land lost to water logging and salinity; and improving the institutional capacity to manage, operate, and maintain the water infrastructure.

Table 4.2 shows the areas covered by the Bank's investment operations during the CAE period.

Table 4.1: Water and Rural Development Projects

Sectors	Number of projects	Amount ($ millions)	% Distribution
Water resources	7	666.0	57.0
Agriculture	3	436.0	38.0
Rural development	3	59.4	5.0
Total commitments	**13**	**1,161.4**	**100**

Source: World Bank project documents.

Table 4.2: Contributions of Water Management Projects, Fiscal 1999–2006

		% Distribution	
Category	**Area covered/served (feddan)**	**Bank**	**Egypt, Arab Rep. of**
Irrigation	850,084	12.4	10.6
Drainage	1,905,000	27.8	23.8
Pumping stations	4,100,000	59.8	51.3
Bank program total	6,855,084	100.0	85.7
Cultivated land	8,000,000	—	100.0

Sources: CAPMAS and internal World Bank project documents.
Note: Total cultivated land for Egypt is about 8 million feddan (3.36 million hectares).

Through its water sector operations, the Bank covered an aggregate area of close to 6.8 million feddan out of a total cultivated area of some 8 million feddan (3.36 million hectares).

The Bank's irrigation projects have played a central role in the sector. The Irrigation Improvement Project (1994) completed water delivery systems for 68 branch and sub-branch canals serving 210,000 feddan. The follow-up operation, the Integrated Irrigation Improvement and Management Project (2005), improved the irrigation system serving an area of 550,000 feddan. Finally, the West Delta Water Conservation and Irrigation Rehabilitation Project (2007) aims to provide a surface water supply system covering about 90,084 feddan, an area formerly served by private groundwater development, which has depleted the aquifer. The total area served by the Bank-financed irrigation investments thus covers about 11 percent of Egypt's cultivated area.

In the Bank's two drainage projects during the CAE review period, a total of 1,905,000 feddan of irrigated farmland (about one-quarter of the total cultivated area) were targeted for improved technical design and system management. The first project provided new subsurface drainage infrastructure for 590,000 feddan and rehabilitated the drainage system for an additional 150,000 feddan, bringing the total covered area to 740,000 feddan. The second drainage project covered a total area of 1,165,000 feddan, consisting of new subsurface drainage and rehabilitation of older subsurface drainage systems.

The Bank has also financed the rehabilitation and rebuilding of 174 pumping stations, serving an aggregate area of 4.1 million feddan. That is slightly more than half the total cultivated area in Egypt. This was mainly achieved through two projects during the CAE period. The Second Pumping Stations Rehabilitation Project (1990, completed during the period under review) rehabilitated 70 pumping stations serving approximately 1.7 million feddan. The Third Pumping Stations Rehabilitation Project (1998) helped rehabilitate 104 pumping stations that serve an aggregate area of 2.4 million feddan. An additional 533,000 feddan were to be served by the construction of 21 new pumping stations, but this has not materialized yet because of implementation delays. These Bank projects also provided support for strengthening the Mechanical and Electrical Department of the Ministry of Public Works and Water Resources.

Agricultural development

The Bank repeatedly tried to improve rural credit but was never successful. As mentioned above, the $300 million Private Sector and Agriculture Development Project was canceled some four years after approval, primarily because of a lack of commitment by the implementing agency, the Principal Bank for Development and Agricultural Credit. Another project, the Agricultural Modernization Project, failed to improve rural finance intermediation but did manage to create agricultural employment and technology transfer.

The objectives of the East Delta Agricultural Services Project were to provide support services to facilitate the settlement and increase agricultural production by settling about 26,000 low-income families on about 130,000 feddans of recently developed lands in the East Delta. The implementation progress has been notably slow, which could indicate that the Bank did not fully anticipate the technical and social complexity of implementing this project, especially when it came to developing financial support services.

Rural development

The Bank's rural development lending portfolio was relevant in its objectives, which were well aligned with the government's own approach to the issues, although Bank lending in rural development was limited both in number of operations and in volume. The two projects implemented during the CAE period are the Matruh Resource Management Project (1993, $22 million) and the Sohag Rural Development Project (1998, $25 million).

The Matruh project had the following objectives: to conserve water and land resources and simultaneously reduce poverty and improve the quality of life of the targeted beneficiaries (Bedouins). The project was innovative in that it was the first attempt by the Bank in Egypt to engage communities in addressing their own developmental challenges. IEG rated the project satisfactory, based on achievements in areas such as water harvesting and increases in the welfare of participating households. A follow-up Matruh Two Project (2003) was canceled in 2005 at the request of the government, two years after approval.

The Sohag Rural Development Project started to address regional disparities by focusing on a poor governorate in Upper Egypt. The Sohag Project aims to improve the capacity of rural communities to plan, implement, operate, and maintain infrastructure investments. The project is progressing well according to the supervision reports and could, if successful, represent a promising avenue for replication and upscaling.

Bank knowledge products provided the strong analytical underpinnings of the Bank's engagement in the rural and water resources sectors, although some of them had no operational follow-up. The agricultural export strategy, for example, was meant to precede a major operation that did not materialize because of lack of interest by Egyptian officials. In the water resources management sector, however, the analytical work feeds into the Bank's lending portfolio, as illustrated by the irrigation, pumping, and drainage projects during the review period. The Bank wrote a paper on cost-effectiveness and equity in Egypt's water sector as part of the PER, which government officials and other donors noted had a substantial impact on the preparation of the government budget and investment program in the sector.

Outcomes

Significant progress has been made in rehabilitating and restructuring the water resources infrastructure, including major institutional reforms.

Improvements in irrigation systems

The Bank-financed irrigation projects introduced buried pipe tertiary canals (under pressure) to replace open tertiaries with a single pumped lift to raise the water into the tertiary and to provide the pressure needed to irrigate from below. The new technology has eliminated the chaos, wastage, and inequity among farmers. The projects have introduced the concept of continuous flow in all levels of canals, rather than the old system of time-concentrated large flows and overirrigation, followed by complete cut-off of large sections. The introduction of this practice, more complex in practice than initially conceived, has been only partially achieved in the Bank's project areas in the Nile Delta, but even the progress so far is an important contribution to the process.

Expansion and modernization of drainage systems

At the national level, the area covered by drainage infrastructure increased from 4.9 million feddan in 1999 to 5.4 million feddan in 2004. Egypt has become a world leader in the field, and laser-leveled construction and installation of pipe tile drains have become the norm throughout the country.

Increase in production and yields

Agricultural productivity has improved for major crops, such as cotton, wheat, rice, and broad beans, ranging from 10 to 20 percent between 1998–99 and 2004–05. A 2005 Food and Agricultural Organization study confirmed that average crop yields in the irrigation and drainage rehabilitated areas were cotton at 2.4 tons per hectare, rice at 6.5 tons per hectare, wheat at 4.3 tons per hectare, and beans at 2.4 tons per hectare. There were also changes in the cropping patterns and a 6–10 percent increase in farmers' incomes.

Capacity building

Bank operations, in cooperation with Germany and the Netherlands, built significant capacity within the Egyptian Authority for Public Drainage Projects. Training improved skills, not only within the government but also among private sector contractors. Innovation was fostered, and drainage implementation now benefits from a geographic information system, laser land leveling and controls, and state-of-the-art drainage pipe installation. Most important, a viable monitoring and evaluation system was established and is working well to identify and prioritize new works as well as to monitor the impacts of investments.

Institutional development and cost recovery

As many as 3,000 water users' associations established under the Irrigation Improvement Project serve as an excellent example of the effect of user involvement and cooperation on the system's management. The water users' associations have taken over operations and maintenance responsibilities for the tertiary-level irrigation system. The Bank's projects have been instrumental (and at the leading edge for both other donors and the government of Egypt nationally) in creating and extending water users' associations, first at the tertiary canal level and more recently to secondary and even main canals, with elected boards and chairpeople.

A new concept with respect to cost recovery is about to be tested in the recently approved (June 2007) West Delta Water Conservation and Irrigation Rehabilitation Project. This is one of the most innovative projects in the water field worldwide and probably the first real public-private partnership in the irrigation field anywhere. A private sector operator will be chosen to design, build, and operate the irrigation system, with a capital contribution by this operator and by farmers who sign up for connection to water. These farmer contracts plus the operator's equity are expected to ensure that all capital costs of the project will be recovered, as will operation and maintenance costs based on volume of water received by each farmer.

The agriculture sector has performed well during the CAE period. Agricultural production has grown substantially, with 33 and 40 percent increases reported for wheat and maize production, respectively. Agriculture value added grew at a rate of 3.5 percent per annum between 1995 and 2005. The sector accounted for 13.9 percent of GDP in 2005. The value of Egyptian agricultural exports grew between 2000 and 2005 by 121 percent, compared to an 11 percent increase in agricultural imports. This improvement is due mainly to increases in horticultural exports, making it one of the strongest subsectors in Egyptian agriculture.

However, there was no progress in reducing the disparities in living standards between Lower Egypt and Upper Egypt. The poverty headcount grew to 18.6 percent in urban Upper Egypt from 11 percent, and in the rural area it increased from 29 percent to 39 percent between 1996 and 2005. In contrast, during the same period for the country as a whole, the poverty headcount was stable, with just under 20 percent of the population falling below the poverty line; poverty incidence fell in rural Lower Egypt, where most of the Bank-financed water management and agriculture investment were located. Thus, whereas Bank projects may have been successful in lowering poverty in Lower Egypt, they had no impact on poverty differentials between Lower and Upper Egypt.

Assessing the Bank's contribution

The objectives of the Bank's assistance strategy were relevant to the country's needs and consistent with government strategies. The Bank's rural program relied heavily on investments in water resources management and was instrumental in improving Egypt's water infrastructure. The Bank was widely acknowledged as the leader of the donor community in this area, and its contribution is significant. The largely renewed irrigation system is the platform on which the recent boom in commercial agriculture and exports has stood, and the Bank has had a significant role in this.

Outside of irrigation, drainage, and pumping, the Bank tried to spur Egyptian agricultural sector growth and exports through analytical work and lending for rural finance, but the lending was not successful. Nevertheless, the Bank did continue to engage in dialogue with the government of Egypt on rural poverty, which culminated in solid analytical studies that can form the basis of future assistance.

Infrastructure

Background

There was a significant reduction of public investment in the late 1990s in Egypt. That reduction helped restrain fiscal deficits, but it also may have compromised the infrastructure base on which the growth potential of the economy and private investment relies. Infrastructure investment needs remain substantial. Approximately 4–6 percent of GDP needs to be invested annually in infrastructure in the Middle East and North Africa Region to satisfy the requirements of new investment, as well as maintenance and replacement spending. The decline in investment in the Middle East and North Africa, including Egypt, is reported to have compromised the infrastructure base, which is further challenged by the high growth in demand for modern infrastructure services.

The Bank's objectives and program

The Bank's objectives in the energy, telecommunication, and transportation sectors were twofold. First, the Bank sought to help the government increase the involvement of the private sector in public infrastructure investments. Second, the Bank aimed to help improve the policy and regulatory framework for the telecommunications sector. The assistance strategy in 1997 allocated $400 million in IBRD guarantees against private participation in infrastructure. The 2001 CAS aimed to support the authorities' efforts to develop the regulatory framework for the telecommunications sector and to modernize the strategy, structure, processes, and systems of the Egyptian postal services.

The 2005 CAS presents a much different picture for infrastructure sectors. Although private sector participation is still a main theme and assistance to improve the policy and regulatory framework is extended to the energy and transport sectors, the CAS adds direct support for *public* investment to increase power generation and improve transportation (ports, roads, railways, and urban transportation).

After an active infrastructure program from 1959 to the early 1990s, the Bank left the infrastructure sector completely in the mid-1990s. After disagreements on tariffs and financial management, the fiscal 1992 Kureimat Power Project was closed after two years and $199 million of the $220 million loan was canceled (large cofinanciers provided well over $1 billion to the project). That effectively ended the Bank's lending role in the power subsector, even though it did provide advisory services. In other infrastructure sectors, the Bank's absence lasted even longer, partly because of the presence of other large cofinanciers, such as USAID, with grant funds, and the EU, but also partly due to the government's preference for private sector provision of infrastructure.

In the power sector, the government approved plans to open power generation to independent power producers (IPPs) in 1996. The government strategy at that time was to encourage private sector financing. IFC played a prominent role in providing advisory services and financing to these IPPs. However, with the devaluation of the Egyptian pound in the early 2000s, the cost of the power purchased—which is fixed in U.S. dollars—started to exceed the average retail price for electricity, thus bringing losses to the sector (see box 4.1).

In the telecommunications sector, the government undertook a major reform program by creating the Telecommunications Regulatory Authority, introducing a new legal framework to liberalize the sector, and recruiting advisors for the partial privatization of Telecom Egypt. The Bank prepared a project to support this reform. However, the government decided in 2002 to continue these reforms with USAID's support, and the Bank loan was dropped shortly before Board approval. Most of the reforms were implemented in the 2002–05 period.

The event that changed the Bank program in infrastructure—and with it the entire image of the Bank among the Egyptian political elite, and hence the role of the Bank in Egyptian development—was a request from senior Egyptian authorities to finance an airport development project in 2003. The request was conditional on the Bank's commitment to rapid decision making, project preparation, and project approval, which was both obtained and fulfilled.[1]

The Airports Development Project was not planned in the 2001 CAS, but it was consistent with criteria set out in the CAS for Bank financing: there was strong government commitment and support for a project, and the Bank would be adding value to an operation through its involvement. The 2001 CAS was reviewed by the Board prior to events of September 11, 2001, when concessions were still the favored option for developing infrastructure. Following the September 11 events, investment flows to Egypt declined—as support for all airlines lessened—while the need for expanding transportation

Box 4.1: Egypt's Independent Power Projects

In 1996, the government approved plans to open power generation to IPPs to construct and operate new power plants in the 650–700 megawatt (MW) range, all fired by natural gas. Three projects—Sidi Krir, Port Said, and Suez—were tendered as a start-up program, to be followed by 15 more. The large size of the program stimulated great interest; being one of the pioneers was seen as an advantage. The bidding was intensely competitive, with more than 50 firms expressing interest at the prequalification stage. The first IPP, Sidi Krir, was won by Intergen (a joint venture of Shell and Bechtel), and the other two were won by Electricité de France. IFC offered both direct financing and syndication services for all three IPPs, but eventually its offer was taken up only by the Electricité de France plants. IFC loaned $90 million directly to the two projects and arranged (with Barclays Bank and Société Générale) a total of $405 million more of syndicated loans, including $100 million from the John Hancock Life Insurance Company. The power purchasing agreement specified that Egyptian Electric Holding Company payments be made in U.S. dollars (with a Central Bank guarantee), with a formula to adjust fuel costs in Egyptian pounds; so Egyptian Electric Holding Company bore the exchange risks.

All three IPPs, with a total capacity of 2,048 MW and representing about 8 percent of total installed capacity, have remained in force according to the original contracts through a major currency devaluation and through the sale of the two Electricité de France plants to a Malaysian conglomerate, and of Sidi Krir. The Malaysian government—a Saudi Arabian partner—then bought Sidi Krir also, putting all three IPPs under Malaysian control in March 2006. All three plants have continued to supply power to the grid cheaply (about 2.5 U.S. cents per kilowatt hour—about the same rate as state-owned plants also receiving highly subsidized natural gas). The government honored its 3 IPP contracts but stopped the 12 additional planned IPPs and modified the requirements. New projects were required to obtain foreign currency financing abroad, involve the local private sector in project construction and operation, pay local costs in local currency, and have power customers—not the Egyptian Electric Holding Company—sign power purchasing agreements. No new IPPs were undertaken.

Source: Eberhard and Gratwick (2007) and IEG CAE mission.

facilities continued to rise. Finally, the project was consistent with the Bank's emerging Infrastructure Action Plan, which called for more responsiveness to client demands for infrastructure in light of the private sector's declining ability and interest in financing public-purpose infrastructure.

The government's request from the Bank was fourfold: (i) provide experience in financing large and complex transportation infrastructure projects, as well as knowledge of associated development issues; (ii) ensure proper consideration of environmental and social issues; (iii) enhance chances of attracting high-quality bids for private management contracts through transparent tendering; and (iv) assist transport liberalization.

The Airports Development Project was prepared quickly. The appraisal took place in January 2004; Bank approval (of a $335 million loan) was on March 30, 2004, signing on March 31, 2004, parliamentary ratification in June 2004, and beginning of disbursement on August 24, 2004. Construction started in December of that same year. These events, which are normally distributed across more than two years for Bank projects in Egypt, essentially followed the pattern of the Bank's better emergency disaster operations. This impressive performance, together with the advent of a reform-minded government, was the cornerstone of a profound change in the relationship between Egypt and the Bank.

Implementation progressed unusually well by both Egyptian and Bank standards. A new terminal at Sharm El Sheikh Airport was completed in May 2007 and opened to commercial traffic in June 2007. The third terminal at Cairo International Airport was mostly completed as well. Institutional development initiatives on liberalizing air transport, developing an air cargo strategy, and building management capacity have been with technical committees for the implementation arrangements. As of November 2007, only a little more than three years after disbursement began, the project had disbursed about 80 percent of total commitment.

The early success of the Airports Development Project encouraged the authorities to request financing for a major new power plant. The El Tebbin Power Project was approved in 2006 for $270 million to finance a 700 MW power plant comprising two units using natural gas as a main fuel. This project is part of the government's new power generation expansion program. The Egyptian Electricity Holding Company, responsible for generation, transmission, and distribution of electricity in Egypt, developed a generation expansion plan for the 2002–07 period, during which 4,500 MW of combined-cycle gas turbines would be added to the generation capacity. The project has a TA component to address key issues facing the electricity sector, such as the need for better financial performance, strengthening the pricing structure, and energy efficiency. Project implementation is proceeding smoothly.

After 2005, the Bank started to provide advisory services on broad energy issues. It arranged an international conference in September 2005 on demand-side management and energy efficiency and a study on the economic costs of natural gas (Economic Consulting Associates 2007), and another on the development of a load management program and design of time of use/seasonal pricing have been delivered. These studies were well received by Egyptian authorities and are shaping the energy policy of the country. An energy pricing strategy study is under way.

The Bank returned to the telecommunication sector in June 2006 with a reimbursable TA program to provide advisory services on telecom development and regulation, postal development, and information technology development. This program is the continuation of earlier reforms and includes the establishment of a postal policy unit in the Ministry of Communication and Information Technology, analysis of the economic impact of telecommunication liberalization, and enhancement of the regulatory and institutional framework.

Outcomes

Energy sector

The most notable progress in the energy sector has been physical expansion. Installed power generation capacity stood at 20,452 MW in 2006, of which 75 percent was based on locally produced gas. Most of the remaining power was hydroelectric, mainly from the Aswan Dam. The increase in electricity demand has averaged about 7 percent per year during the CAE period. There were no chronic supply shortages in Egypt. Per capita electricity consumption increased from 912 kilowatt hours (kWh) per head in 1999 to 1,312 kWh in 2006.

In the late 1990s, energy was unbundled. Generation, transmission, and distribution/retailing segments were functionally separated within the Egyptian Electricity Holding Company, a state-owned holding company. A sector regulator, the Egyptian Electric Utilities and Consumer Protection Authority, was established in 2000; its role has been limited, particularly in advising on or setting prices. The Bank has been helping the authorities strengthen the regulatory framework by providing international experience. Although positive steps have been taken, the legal and regulatory framework remains unfinished.

Underpricing of energy has been a problem for the country since the early 1990s and remains so today. Egyptian electricity prices are low by international standards and relative to a number of other countries in the Region. Electricity prices were changed in October 2004 (from an average of 12.8 piastres [100 piastres = 1 Egyptian pound]/kWh—2.2 cents—to 14.06 piastres/kWh—2.4 cents) for the first time since 1992. Electricity prices were increased at an average rate of 8.6 percent in 2004, by 5 percent in 2005, and by 7.5 percent in 2006. A further 5 percent per year increase is planned for the next five years.

The prices of gasoline, diesel, fuel oil, and natural gas increased in 2004 and 2006. The Ministry of Finance started to record energy subsidies in the budget in 2005–06 to increase transparency. In August 2007, the government announced plans to eliminate gas and electricity subsidies for energy-intensive industries over the coming three years to help reduce budget deficits.

Telecommunications

The reform process started in 1998 with the establishment of an independent regulatory authority and the incorporation of the government-owned operator, Telecom Egypt. A new telecommunications law was passed in 2003. Although Telecom Egypt is still the sole provider of fixed-line telephones, the government recently sold a 20 percent stake in the company through an international public offering on the Cairo and Alexandria Stock Exchange and the London Stock Exchange. The number of fixed lines in operation increased from 4.7 million lines in 1998 to 11.4 million in 2006, raising penetration to 15 percent. Egypt has two mobile networks operated by private firms. The government auctioned a third mobile phone operator license in July 2006 for $2.9 billion. The number of mobile subscribers increased from 177,000 to 17.7 million between 1998 and 2006. The mobile penetration rate reached 24 percent.

Transport sector

Egypt's transport sector has been characterized by limited new investments, neglect of essential maintenance, inefficient labor and noncommercial practices resulting in severe bottlenecks, poor safety standards, and low service levels. The national rail system is the oldest in the Region, and the government has launched an investment program to modernize both track and trains. The modernization program was made more urgent by two train crashes in 2006, which exposed the degree of decay of the rail network. The government introduced new legislation in June 2006 allowing private sector investment in the railway sector for the first time.

In air services, major civil aviation reforms have been under way, including gradual liberalization of air transport and private sector participation in airport services management. The third terminal at Cairo Airport, scheduled to open in 2008, will be able to handle 11 million passengers per year, twice as many as before. A new terminal has opened in Sharm El Sheikh, increasing capacity from 2.5 million to 4 million passengers per year. The state-owned carrier, Egypt Air, has been restructured and its service quality has improved in recent years.

Assessing the Bank's contribution

The Bank's presence in the infrastructure sector has varied, and therefore its contribution has been mixed. In the power sector, the Bank has only recently resumed its lending support after more than 12 years' absence, and it is still too soon to assess outcomes of this support. However, it did provide advisory services to the IPPs. Increased capacity is attributable in part to the Bank Group, although IFC had a larger role in this than the Bank. The recent focus on energy pricing and subsidies has also benefited from Bank input.

In telecommunications, the Bank prepared a project that included a program of reform; although the project was ultimately financed by USAID, the Bank should get some credit for recent reforms that increased services. Finally, although the Bank can be credited with supporting the expanded capacity of airports and reforms in civil aviation, whether the large Bank loan addressed poverty directly enough remains debatable.

Perhaps most significant, however, the Bank has earned a position as a trusted advisor to government officials in a number of key infrastructure subsectors. Egyptian officials told the IEG mission of their admiration for the quality of Bank project preparation and policy advice, which suggests that the Bank will continue to make important contributions to reforms.

Environment

The degradation of air quality in greater Cairo and other metropolitan cities has been a serious environmental issue. Major contributors to air pollution have been the burning of agricultural residues and municipal waste, public and private transport, lead smelters, fertilizers, and cement factories. The second major environmental issue has been water pollution. As noted earlier, Egypt's most obvious vulnerability in terms of its natural resource endowment lies in its extreme dependence on the Nile. High population growth and strong economic activity in the 1990s; high levels of water abstraction, particularly for irrigation; and large pollution loads discharged into the river and into irrigation canals and water drainage systems have created major problems for downstream users, including farmers who recycle polluted water for both irrigation and human consumption.

Activities in Egypt's coastal areas are vital for the national economy. Together with the oil industry and income from the Suez Canal, tourism has been one of the top foreign exchange earners in the country, amounting to an estimated $4.5 billion in 2000. Until the early 1980s, tourism had been concentrated along the Mediterranean coast between Alexandria in the West Delta to Port Said in the East Delta, primarily for vacationing Egyptians. Tourism has since expanded to new regions along the Mediterranean Coast, and the Red Sea Coast has provided attractions for international tourists. This growth in tourism activity has put tremendous pressure on Egypt's coastal resources, with numerous ecological threats.

The Bank's objectives and program

Three priority areas of Bank strategy in environment have been preservation of natural and particularly marine resources, reduction of urban and industrial pollution to improve water and air quality, and monitoring and enforcing the environment protection law and its regulations. The 2001 CAS indicated that an assessment of the costs of environmental degradation at a national level would be crucial to help raise awareness. The 2005 CAS reemphasized the importance of improved water resource management in Egypt and noted that it is a priority issue for the government as well. The Bank's support under the CAS was intended to continue to focus on helping improve water and wastewater quality, sanitation services, and water demand management.

The Bank approved only two projects under the Environment Sector Board during the CAE period: the First and Second Egypt Pollution Abatement Projects (EPAP and EPAP II), approved in 1997 and 2006, respectively. The Red Sea Coastal and Marine Resource Management Project, financed by the Global Environment Facility and approved in 1993, was being implemented. Total commitment for these three projects was $59.8 million, representing only 2 percent of total Bank commitments to Egypt during the period under review.

The first EPAP, a loan of $35 million, had several goals:

- Strengthen the monitoring and enforcement capabilities of environmental institutions.
- Establish technical and financial mechanisms for supporting pollution-abatement investments in greater Cairo, Alexandria, Suez, and Ismailia.
- Support environmental audit programs.
- Promote awareness and media education programs.

The EPAP provided financing to 25 subprojects in 21 enterprises (10 of which were public enterprises) for pollution-related improvements, including emissions reduction, wastewater treatment, and solid waste management. The operation originally intended to finance investments in heavy industries that posed the greatest health and environmental risks, but a creditworthiness requirement for potential subborrowers eliminated the eligibility of many state-owned enterprises—which included the major polluters—and reoriented assistance toward subsidizing viable private firms. In terms of the institutional capacity, the project did help the Egyptian Environmental Affairs Agency (EEAA) improve its technical expertise and overall capacity.

EPAP II ($20 million), cofinanced by the major donors in Egypt (European Investment Bank, Kreditanstalt für Wiederaufbau [a German government-owned development bank], DANIDA, Japan, and France), incorporated lessons from the first project. However, IEG questions whether all relevant lessons have been adequately taken into account. Specifically, EPAP II continues to rely on directed credit lines to industrial enterprises for pollution-abating investments, although this design proved problematic in the previous project in Egypt as well as in Brazil, India, and China (IEG 2008a).

The Red Sea and Gulf of Aden contain some of the world's most important coastal and marine environments and resources. The Red Sea coast is one of the country's major tourism areas, with a large potential for tourism expansion. The Red Sea Coastal and Marine Resource Management Project, approved in 1993, was under implementation until 2002. The implementing agencies were Egypt's Ministry of Tourism, Tourism Development Authority, EEAA, and Red Sea Governorate. The project achieved its overall objectives by developing and implementing policies, plans, and regulations that ensured the sustainable environmental management of marine coastal resources of the Red Sea. It also collected and interpreted crucial information needed to manage resources and implement a coastal zone management plan. An environment unit has been established in the Tourism Development Authority, and EEAA fully enforces the environmental impact assessment regulations for tourism development. IEG rated the outcome of the project as satisfactory.

The Bank has carried out several studies. The cost assessment of environmental degradation (World Bank 2002a) is an almost seminal paper in Egypt, one of the very few tailored to this subject. The study, however, was not broadly disseminated or discussed with the government, so it did not have an impact on the government's agenda for environmental policy. The Bank also completed a country environmental analysis (World Bank 2005a) that articulated policy recommendations for the near future.

Outcomes

Progress in meeting environmental objectives has been mixed, and a large agenda remains.

Table 4.3: Environment Outcome Indicators

	Baseline 1998–99	Outcome 2004–05
Air pollution		
Electricity production from natural gas sources (% of total)	48.5	70.8
Electricity production from oil sources (% of total)	32.1	16.2
CO_2 emissions (000 kilo tonnes)	121.5	139.6
CO_2 emissions (metric tons per capita)	1.9	2.0
PM10, country level (micrograms per m^3)[a]	160.5	134.8
Water pollution		
Organic water pollutant (BOD) emissions (kg per day per worker)	0.20	0.20
Organic water pollutant (BOD) emissions (000 kg per day)	203.6	186.1
Nile water pollution annual average		
Dissolved oxygen (must not be less than 5 mg/liter)	6.6	6.6
Chemical oxygen demand (must be no more than 10 mg/liter)	13.4	12.0
Biological oxygen demand (must be no more than 6 mg/liter)	3.8	3.6

Sources: World Development Indicators and CAPMAS.
Note: BOD = biological oxygen demand.
a. Urban population-weighted PM10 micrograms per cubic meter.

Water quality in the Nile north of Cairo and in the delta branches improved slightly between 2000 and 2005, judging from data presented in the State of Environment Report. In the case of organic loads expressed as biological oxygen demand and chemical oxygen demand, the improvement was sufficient to shift the water quality measures to within national standards. Meanwhile, the increasing volumes of treated wastewater were used to irrigate forest tree crops rather than being dumped into the Nile, an approach that seems to suit local cultural and religious sensitivities.

Air quality indicators have started to improve, according to the 2005 Egypt State of Environment Report (see table 4.3). A number of causes are cited: (i) eliminating leaded gasoline in Egypt; (ii) gradually converting most fixed power generation, industrial processes, and housing to natural gas, Egypt's most plentiful energy resource; (iii) using the armed forces as a contractor to collect and compress rice straw to be recycled into either fertilizer or animal feed, as an alternative to burning; (iv) collecting municipal and agricultural wastes, otherwise burned, in covered landfills and other types of dumps; (v) using a subsidized credit line to reduce industrial emissions; and (vi) implementing special monitoring and enforcement programs for cement plants and lead smelters. In general, air quality in 2005 was markedly better than in 1998, particularly in areas where the Bank program was active.

Monitoring and enforcement have been strengthened some since 2003. Evidence indicates that with the contributions of EPAP, the enforcement capabilities of the central EEAA units were enhanced in carrying out pollution inventories, environmental inspections, and audits and enforcement activities and thus improving the ability of these entities to carry out their legal responsibilities under the Environment Protection Law. However, the complex scheme of authority between the federal level and governorates, and between the EEAA and other line ministries, has undermined the system's effectiveness. The capacity of sector ministries to deal with environmental issues and the mechanisms of coordination with EEAA vary according to the relevance of environmental issues for the respective sector.

There has also been progress in the protection of biodiversity. When the 1993 Red Sea Coastal and Marine Resource Management Project started, funded by the Global Environment Facility, there was only one small protected area on the entire Red Sea Coast. The size of protected area reached 35,000 square kilometers by mid-2007, in a long series of parks and reserves down to the Sudan border. The entire coast is now subject to environmental management and patrolling, including professional assessment of environmental impact for any significant development. Responsibility for protection of reefs from tourist damage has been assigned to nearby major hotels.

Assessing the Bank's contribution

Despite its limited direct lending assistance to the environment, the Bank has contributed improvements in outcomes, monitoring, and enforcement. The Bank has produced two major analytical reports and cooperated well with other major donors, Denmark, Germany, Japan, the UNDP, and USAID. Bank analytical work (for example, estimating the costs of environmental degradation and, most recently, a Country Environmental Analysis) has been very good at helping Egyptian authorities understand the nature and importance of environmental problems, especially with respect to metropolitan air quality.

Nevertheless, the Bank has not played a major role in strengthening environmental institutions in Egypt in part because of the relative importance of other—mainly bilateral—donors and the wide availability of grant resources to fund interventions in support of this area. Looking forward, the EEAA and enforcement of pollution legislation need to be further strengthened, and decentralization of environmental management activities needs to be completed.

Summary

The outcomes of the second pillar of Bank assistance are rated *satisfactory* (see table 4.4). Physical achievements and project outputs in most operations were satisfactory, and institutions were strengthened. Water users' associations became operational, with effective involvement in water resources management. The government has begun to implement its Integrated Water Resources Plan. Agriculture sector growth and export performances were impressive during the review period, likely because of the Bank's support for irrigation and drainage. In contrast, there was no progress in reducing living standards differences between Upper and Lower Egypt, despite contributions to improved living standards in areas served by the Bank's two small rural development projects (Matruh and Sohag).

In the infrastructure sectors (transportation, energy, and telecommunications), outcomes were good. In the energy sector, installed power generation increased and chronic shortages were allayed. Energy reforms are now under way, including unbundling and some regulatory strengthening. A large agenda remains. Energy

Table 4.4: Pillar 2: Summary Outcome Rating

Objective	Outcomes
Improving water resources management, infrastructure, and environment	**Satisfactory**
Improving water resources management, agriculture, and rural development	Satisfactory
Infrastructure	Satisfactory
Environment	Moderately satisfactory

Source: IEG.

prices remain heavily subsidized. The telecommunications sector has been liberalized, allowing private mobile operators and expanding (mainly mobile) telephone service dramatically. Airport capacity has been significantly increased, thus reducing a potential barrier to tourism.

In environment, air and water quality are beginning to improve. In addition, the EEAA has been empowered; although environmental monitoring and enforcement have been improved, the complex lines of authority weaken the system.

Chapter 5

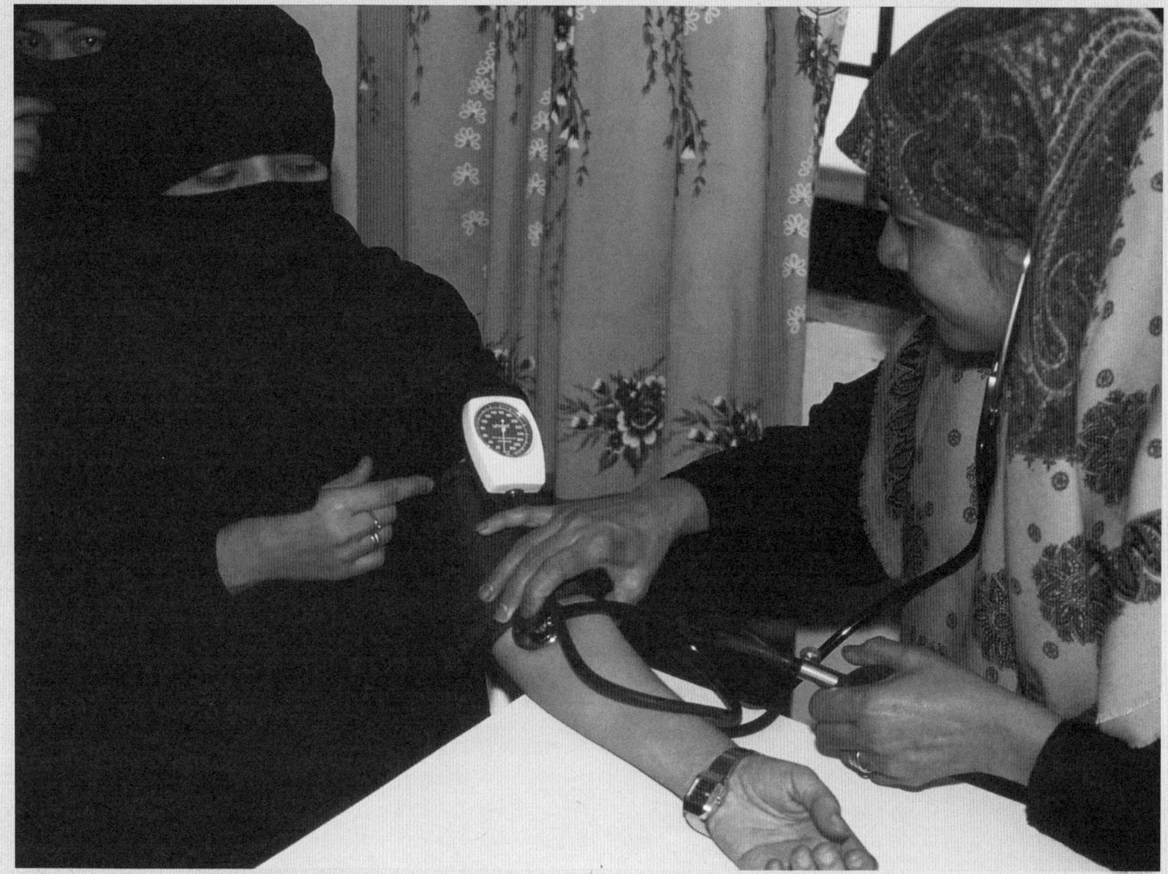

Much progress was made during the review period on both health and gender issues, as can be seen here, with a Muslim woman having her blood pressure taken. Photo by Curt Carnemark, courtesy of the World Bank Photo Library.

Human Development and Poverty Reduction

The Bank consistently supported poverty reduction and human development in all three CASs covering the review period. The strategies focused on several priority objectives: (i) improving equity—enhancing access to education and health services in remote poor areas, access of girls to education, and effective social safety nets; (ii) enhancing quality of education and health services at all levels; and (iii) enhancing efficiency and sustainability of public expenditure, health insurance, and subsidies and social safety nets.

Bank instruments consisted of considerable economic and sector work, combined with relatively limited new lending. A noteworthy aspect of the analytical effort has been the recent agreement on several subjects for reimbursable TA (pension and social assistance reforms). The lending program in part reflected Egypt's transition from an IDA-eligible low-income country to a lower-middle-income country. Several ongoing projects were completed during the CAE period. The new lending targeted mainly education and training, with a little for social protection, but no new lending for health, nutrition, and population.

Gender

Background

At the beginning of the review period, Egypt had significant gender disparities. Women were in principle protected by a number of laws and policies, but implementation was inconsistent. Traditional practices such as early marriage and female genital mutilation were persistent issues. In education, girls' enrollment ratios were 5–10 percent lower than boys' at each level of the system (table 5.1). Youth literacy for males was 83 percent; for females it was 72 percent. Literacy for males 10 and older was 71 percent but for females only 49 percent; the rural gap was twice the urban one. Some reasons for these disparities were parental social concerns and biases, costs of education, low quality of education, few female teachers, and stereotyping.

In health, females' life expectancy exceeded males' by four years, as in many other countries. In employment, the female labor participation rate was low (constituting just 20 percent of the labor force), and unemployment rates for women were much higher than for men. Only 2 percent of Parliament members were female.

Table 5.1: Gender Indicators (percent)

	Baseline 1996–98	Outcome 2004–05
Education		
Primary gross enrollment ratio (M/F)	107/94	104/97
Secondary gross enrollment ratio (M/F)	80/70	89/82
Youth literacy (15–24) (M/F)	83/72	90/79
Adult literacy (15+) (M/F)	67/44	83/59
Health and population		
Life expectancy at birth (M/F)	65/69	68/72
Employment		
Female share of nonagricultural labor force	20	22
Society		
Female % of seats in Parliament	2	2

Sources: UNDP, World Bank, and CAE mission.

The Bank's objectives and program

The 1997 CAS offered no explicit strategy regarding gender, but operations were expected to support reducing the gender gap in education. The Bank's strategy was to focus on AAA aimed at addressing the key gender-related issues and on developing mechanisms to mainstream gender in Egypt's next five-year plan. The strategy in the 2005 CAS was to support formation of women's groups in development activities; build capacity for community organizations; investigate barriers to women's entrepreneurship; and build capacity for mainstreaming gender, in addition to continued special attention to gender concerns in education. The CAS frameworks had many indicators, with the quantitative ones being specific annual growth rates of girls' and boys' enrollments and increases in female economic participation.

The Bank's program of nonlending services was extensive. A working paper analyzed gender disparities in education. An education sector review included a gender focus, especially on access and enrollments at various levels. The first Institutional Development Fund grant for Egypt enabled the Bank to support capacity building of the new National Council of Women (NCW). But the main instrument for addressing gender issues was the 2003 country gender assessment; there was significant follow-up through a high-level policy forum and subsequent work. Finally, Egypt provided a case study for the Middle East and North Africa Region's fiscal 2008 report on the constraints facing women entrepreneurs (and employees).

Outcomes

Egypt's progress on gender issues during the review period has been considerable. The government integrated gender into its National Socio-Economic Five Year Plan for 2002–07 and in even greater measure for the successor plan just produced. Gender-disaggregated data are still limited, however. On the legal and institutional front, the government created the NCW in 2000, which developed a national gender strategy in 2007 and set up gender units within 20 ministries and all governorates.

In 1996, prior to this review period, the Ministry of Health issued a decree prohibiting the practice of female circumcision, and in mid-2007 the government began another campaign against the slowly diminishing practice. A law in 2000 permitted wives to apply for divorce, albeit renouncing any claim to dowry and financial maintenance. Another law permitted Egyptian women to pass their nationality to their children in cases where the father was not Egyptian. Laws were passed during the period for specialized tribunals and courts for family-related cases. On the representational front, while the proportion of female members of Parliament remained at 2 percent, a constitutional amendment in 2007 prescribed a much higher minimum in the future.

Improving girls' enrollment was a central aim of the Ministry of Education's 1996 Education Enhancement Program, and there was a project for the eradication of female illiteracy in 1998. Strategies were developed for secondary education (2000) and higher education (2001). There was good progress in increasing female participation at all levels in the review period; gender disparities at both primary and secondary levels were reduced substantially. Female literacy increased significantly. Similarly, in health, life expectancy increased for both genders, and women's health and the utilization of maternity-related services improved markedly.

On the labor market, female participation has been increasing, albeit slowly. Female unemployment declined significantly during the review period. However, it remained several times the rate of male unemployment. With the exception of women with university degrees, unemployment rates for females who leave school at all levels remain dramatically higher than for males.

Egypt has been a pioneer in many types of gender work. It has been the most successful country in the Region at integrating gender concerns into economic decision making, with focused attention not just from the first lady but also from the Cabinet.

The Bank's main impact was through the 2003 country gender assessment and a high-level policy forum on gender in 2005, both involving the first lady, the Prime Minister, and many ministers. Many of the country gender assessment's recommendations were implemented, including the nationality law, divorce law, and family court, and more women judges were appointed. The high-level forum led to preparation—with Bank involvement—of the national gender strategy that was developed using the country gender assessment recommendations. The strategy was launched in 2007.

The Bank's inputs have contributed significantly to the present strength of NCW, which is the focal point for the government's gender efforts. NCW's Secretary General stated that the Bank helped put them on the right track from the beginning. NCW now has branches in every governorate. Joint economic and sector work and fellowships for experts have helped introduce and reinforce Egypt's capacity for serious gender work. Several ministries are closely involved in this work.

The Bank's contributions to gender equality through lending were made mainly through the education and health sectors. The education lending stressed girls' access to education and gender ratios and disparities at various levels. The health lending in part promoted health and population services that directly benefit women. Finally, the SFD—by developing local sources of safe water—saved women time that they formerly spent collecting water, increased enrollments in school, and increased access to health and family planning services.

Assessing the Bank's contribution

The Bank carried out high-quality analytical work on gender in Egypt and achieved high-level dissemination, government focus, and involvement in national strategy formulation. It also helped build institutional capacity of the NCW at the national and local levels and financed the narrowing of gender disparities through its lending, especially in education. The Bank's gender work in Egypt has been important not only for Egypt but also for the Bank itself, both in the Middle East and North Africa Region and globally. The country gender assessment in Egypt has served as a model for work in other countries. The Bank's approach has particularly involved provision of the analytic framework for broadening gender work from the purely social to the economic sphere.

Education and Training

Background

By 1996, primary education (grades 1–5) already enjoyed a gross enrollment ratio of 101 percent,[1] somewhat ahead of the Middle East and North Africa average. In a preproject achievement test, 52 percent of fifth-grade pupils passed Arabic and 43 percent passed mathematics. At the secondary level, the gross enrollment ratio was 75 percent, well above the Middle East and North Africa average. General education made up 33 percent of secondary enrollments and vocational education 67 percent. For higher education, the gross enrollment ratio was already 23 percent, again well ahead of the Region's average. Finally, in early childhood education, the gross enrollment ratio by 1999 was 11 percent, but with a wide range among governorates.

The Bank's objectives and program

The 1997 CAS was to continue to concentrate on improving basic education, while expanding dialogue and activities into new areas such as experimentation with innovative delivery models for primary education, development of assessment capacity to measure progress in providing high-quality education, and increasing the market orientation of technical education and vocational training institutes. The strategy in the 2001 CAS was to continue work on basic education, with an added emphasis on early childhood education to improve educational attainment, particularly of disadvantaged population segments.

New lending would aim at making higher education more relevant to the needs of the economy and establishing a viable mechanism for training in entrepreneurial, technical, and managerial skills. In the 2005 CAS, the Bank was to focus on (i) quality, including curriculum relevance, teacher training, standards, and quality assurance processes; (ii) linkages across educational levels and with other sectors; (iii) cost-effectiveness of education spending; (iv) capacity building; and (v) gender concerns. It will continue its support to skills development through an ongoing project.

In 2002 a comprehensive education sector review was completed (World Bank 2002b) and in 2003 a report on strategic options for early childhood education (World Bank 2003). Several policy notes on education were produced starting in 2005 as part of public expenditure work. A new education sector report in 2007 focused on a small number of highly important issues—quality, the "inequality of quality," and efficiency.

During the review period, the Bank completed a Basic Education Improvement Project that had been approved in 1993 and continued approving and supervising a new generation of five "enhancement" projects for individual subsectors. Most were based on project preparation studies by the government and the Bank, sometimes with other donors, rather than on formal sector work. The projects covered all subsectors of education: basic (called Education Enhancement, 1996), secondary (1999), higher (2002), skills development (2003), and early childhood education (2005). As of publication, only the basic education (1993) and education enhancement projects have been completed and are being evaluated.

Outcomes

During the review period, primary and preparatory education were combined into basic education and lengthened by one year (to nine years' compulsory education). Key indicators are in table 5.2. Enrollments in basic education increased from 11.2 million to 11.5 million, or by 3 percent, from 1996–97 to 2005. The gross enrollment ratio in primary stayed at 101 percent. The secondary gross enrollment ratio rose rapidly from 75 to 86 percent. The percentage in general secondary education rose from 33 percent to 39 percent. As mentioned earlier, gender disparities were reduced significantly. Thus, Egypt made good progress in reducing or eliminating the remaining problems of access to school education. There were also useful gains in learning achievement in the first half of the review period in both primary and lower secondary education (table 5.2).

Table 5.2: Education Indicators (percent)

	Baseline 1996	Outcome 2005
Primary gross enrollment ratios (M/F/total)	107/94/101	104/97/101
Achievement grade 5 (Arabic/math)	52/43[a]	59/50[b]
Secondary gross enrollment ratios (M/F/total)	80/70/75	89/82/86
Secondary general enrollments (total)	33	39
Achievement grade 8 (Arabic/math)	56/44[a]	60/49[b]

Sources: UNESCO, World Bank.
a. Represents 1997.
b. Represents 2003–04.

Despite these overall improvements, several types of disparity and inequality remain important. For example, in 2004, adult illiteracy was as high as 44 percent in Upper Egypt and 35 percent in Lower Egypt. Some gender disparities in education also remain, though they have diminished. Finally, there are major differences in enrollment ratios by income quintile: at the secondary level, the range between top and bottom quintiles is 74–44 percent, and in higher education it is from 48 percent to only 9 percent. In international terms, Egypt is in line with the Middle East and North Africa and lower-middle-income country averages. Its total and female statistics for the formal education system compare well, but it lags on preprimary enrollments and on literacy rates.

Access has increased to be almost universal in primary education and to very high levels in secondary education. However, there has been only partial achievement of the quality objectives of curriculum reform and employer input. Reforms of university governance, autonomy, and financing and improvement of education sector policy making and monitoring and evaluation have not been achieved so far.

The sector review and review of childhood education were both of high quality and highly relevant to both policy and operations. However, the public expenditure work, although solid and relevant, has not had obvious impact. The Bank's AAA has nevertheless contributed to almost every topic of reform discussions now taking place in the sector.

The Bank's education lending has made a range of contributions to Egypt's advances in the sector. School construction under Bank-financed projects has contributed 10–20 percent of enrollment increases and has enhanced access, equity, and even quality (by cutting multiple shifts and overcrowded classes). There has been extensive human capital development. Information and communication technology has been widely introduced, including networks of institutions and libraries and subscriptions to tens of thousands of international journals. On the institutional side, a number of Ministry of Education units have been strengthened, and the government has maintained or extended this capacity up to the present.

The projects have also introduced a number of important innovations to Egypt. One of these has been competitive funds for improvement projects in individual institutions, a feature of several projects. Under projects to help girls stay in school, incentives in kind have not been sustained, but other incentives continue, such as exemption from school fees and school meal programs.

Assessing the Bank's contribution

High-quality sector analysis by the Bank has contributed to nearly all aspects of reform implemented or under discussion in the education sector. The Bank has maintained a lending relationship across all subsectors and throughout the review period despite Egypt's graduation from IDA. Thus, it has directly financed a significant proportion of enrollment increases in primary and secondary education and brought about some quality improvements and institutional strengthening. These achievements outweigh the partial achievement of other objectives and reforms.

Finally, it is useful to note that a key minister told the CAE mission that "with the exception of early childhood education, where the first lady is involved, your projects have not been felt." This statement may reflect mainly the frustration of the urban middle class with the quality of secondary education—which often results in expensive private tutoring being necessary for children to compete for limited numbers of places in the better-regarded university faculties or departments—but it may also reflect the fact that Bank education loans have been small.

Health, Nutrition, and Population

Background

By the mid-1990s, Egypt was undergoing rapid improvement in its health status. The total population was 59 million in 1996, and it was growing at 2 percent per annum. The total fertility rate was 3.5 children per woman, associated with 46 percent of women using modern contraceptive methods. The infant mortality rate was 44 per 1,000 live births, and the maternal mortality rate was 84 per 100,000 in the year 2000. Forty-six percent of births were attended by skilled health staff. Thirty percent of children younger than five were moderately or severely stunted due to chronic malnutrition. Seventy-nine percent of children 12–23 months old were fully immunized. Total health expenditures were 3.7 percent of GDP in 1996, with the public share being 1.9 percent of GDP and amounting to $22 per capita.

The Bank's objectives and program

In the 1997 CAS, the Bank addressed several goals:

- Strengthening the Ministry of Health and Population capacity in policy development, sector planning, and governance
- Establishing a decentralized financing and delivery system at the governorate level, including private as well as public providers and autonomous management arrangements
- Developing health manpower
- Developing pharmaceuticals
- Reforming the financing and organization of health insurance.

In the 2001 CAS, the Bank's strategy was to build on its ongoing efforts at reforming the sector, including a strengthened insurance system, continued improvement of management, and decentralization. In the 2005 CAS, the Bank's strategy is to address continuing inequities in access by continuing to help improve the quality and availability of health services and support participatory and community-based interventions targeting behavior change. It will analyze health finance and health insurance reform within wider sector strategy work.

Just before the review period, the Bank, the government, and other donors pulled previous studies of aspects of the health sector into a Health Sector Reform Program report (World Bank 2000). This provided a roadmap for an ambitious long-term reform program. It proposed the establishment of primary health care services ("family health" model), delivering a technically appropriate and cost-effective package of services countrywide and an insurance scheme with universal enrollment to fund the services. It was an early Bank attempt to develop a model for health service delivery and financing for lower-middle-income countries.

There was a working paper on socioeconomic differences in health, nutrition, and population (World Bank 2000). Another analyzed the economics of tobacco (Nassar 2003). Egypt was also included in the Middle East and North Africa Region human development studies between 1999 and 2003, which covered nutrition, reproductive health, HIV/AIDS, and reducing maternal mortality. The progress of the sector reform program was evaluated in 2004. A health sector PER was produced as a policy note as well (World Bank 2006a).

In the review period, there were two overlapping phases of Bank intervention. The first phase comprised two traditional standalone projects approved earlier, which supported specific health programs. These projects, for national schistosomiasis control (1992) and population in Upper Egypt (1996), were completed in the CAE period. The second phase represented a transition to broad-based support of health sector reform and included both lending and nonlending support. The key operation was the innovative Health Sector Reform Program, which attempted to implement the new roadmap. This program was financed almost equally by the government, USAID, the EU, and the Bank. After Egypt's IDA graduation, the government was unwilling to borrow for health, nutrition, and population, and no new lending was approved during the nine-year review period. However, the government has requested a new family health insurance project for fiscal 2008 alongside Bank policy and technical advisory services.

Outcomes

Egypt made strong efforts and achieved considerable successes in this sector during the last decade, as shown in table 5.3. The infant mortality rate continued its steady decline; the maternal mortality rate fell rapidly; and the proportion of children moderately or severely stunted also fell rapidly. The total fertility rate declined and total health expenditures increased strongly to 6.0 percent of GDP. Improved health indicators, including population/family planning and communicable disease control indicators, have thus been achieved.

The 1997 health sector reform program report (World Bank 1997c) provided the intellectual underpinning not only for the Health Sector Reform Program (and other donors' similar efforts), but also for the President of Egypt's long-term sector strategy framework and Bank work on the fiscal 2008 project. The latter is also being informed by the 2004 evaluation of reforms and later public expenditure work.

The schistosomiasis and population projects were both successful and had positive program outcomes. The first helped drastically reduce incidence of the disease from 35 percent to 3 percent in the Nile Delta and elsewhere. The project's focus on a single disease and simple design resulted in a satisfactory outcome and a successful Bank re-entry to the health sector. The population project contributed substantially to increased contraceptive prevalence in Upper

Table 5.3: Health, Nutrition, and Population Indicators

	Baseline 1996–97	Outcome 2005–06
Infant mortality rate (per 1,000)	44	33
Maternal mortality rate (per 100,000)	84	63
Life expectancy (M/F) (years)	65/69	68/72
Children fully immunized (%)	79	89
Children moderately/severely stunted (%)	30	18
Total fertility rate	3.5	3.1
Contraceptive prevalence rate	46	56
Population (millions)	59.3	72.6
Births with skilled health staff (%)	46	74
Health expenditures/GDP (%)	3.7	6.0

Sources: UNDP, World Bank CAE mission.

Egypt by supporting multisectoral, community-based activities in less than 10 percent of all rural villages. The projects were successful although limited in their impact on the whole sector. However, they have proved sustainable. These two projects had less success in capacity building for strategic program management, which was the other main objective of the projects.

The impact of the Bank's support for health sector reform is somewhat limited even after a decade of implementation of the Health Sector Reform Program Project. Its family health service delivery model has only been implemented in two governorates, Alexandria and Menoufia, both in Lower Egypt. After heavy investment in infrastructure by the Bank and software and technical support and training by USAID and EU, the project substantially increased utilization of formerly poorly attended government health facilities (long waiting lists appeared) and greatly increased provider productivity (physician encounters increased from 3 to 16 per day); this was achieved through incentive payments by donors that were channeled through dedicated funds. However, the poor have enrolled only recently, and in only one area, where out-of-pocket payments were abolished. Thus, their access is so far limited. Also, financial sustainability of the model has not yet been demonstrated.

The insurance component of the Health Sector Reform Program never took off. Bank staff involved in the operation viewed it as high risk and high return; they may not have adequately analyzed the political economy and affordability aspects and hence underestimated the risks. Few on the government side were familiar with the rationale for the new approach involving the application of modern economic theory to health.

The Health Sector Reform Program lending has taken too long to implement and to prove whether it is effective. Nevertheless, the ministry has decided to make the family health service the national model for delivery of primary care, albeit with added services designed to improve financial sustainability.

Assessing the Bank's contribution

The 1997 sector report, although produced just before the review period, was comprehensive and bold. However, although its technical (service delivery) part reflected well-established Bank work worldwide (notably the *World Development Report 1993*), its financing part (health insurance) was a pioneering effort for lower-middle-income countries, which was less familiar to country counterparts and was high risk. Other sector work during the period mainly updated the financing theme. Although Egypt's health and fertility indicators improved substantially during the review period, these outcomes reflect both health sector performance and positive developments in factors outside the health sector, including improved economic performance, higher employment rates, and improvements in women's literacy. The Bank's support for health and population was quite limited in its coverage and was complemented by bigger investments in the health system by other donors. As a result, the Bank's contribution has been limited.

Social Safety Nets and Subsidies

Background

Food subsidies in Egypt originated as early as World War II and have fluctuated considerably since then. In the late 1970s one attempt to curtail them provoked riots, which has colored government thinking ever since. Nevertheless, food subsidies were scaled back during the 1990s.

In 1999, three safety net programs accounted for 2 percent of GDP and 4 percent of government expenditures. Eighty-five percent of this—or 1.5 percent of GDP—was for direct subsidies, including 1.0 percent of GDP for the food subsidy program (covering just four major consumption items, notably baladi bread); 2 percent was for mainly cash transfer payments to specific categories of the disadvantaged by the Ministry of Social Affairs; and 13 percent was for the SFD—especially its employment- and development-oriented public works program and community development program.

The food subsidies were equivalent to nearly 40 percent of the poor's caloric intake, raised their real income by about 10 percent, and lifted about 2 percent of the population out of poverty, but a substantial part of the subsidies went to the nonpoor. Other direct subsidies in health, transportation, and agriculture accounted for about 0.5 percent of GDP. The Ministry of Social Affairs' cash transfers benefited about 1 million people. These three types of programs lifted some out of poverty and prevented others from falling into poverty but reached only a small proportion of the poor.

The Bank's objectives and program

The Bank's 1997 CAS was to focus on analytical work on poverty, decentralization of social services delivery, and nongovernmental organizations and on continued operational support to SFD. In the 2001 CAS, the strategy was to continue work on social protection and the social safety net through SFD. In the 2005 CAS, the strategy is to analyze labor markets, complete studying and propose reforms of pensions, study subsidies and the social safety net, and invest further through SFD.

Early in the review period, the Bank worked with the government on two reports, on skills and training and on the social safety net. However, it is not clear that these produced much action. One working paper analyzed structural adjustment, demography, and the labor market in the 1990s; another studied the distributional impact of food subsidies. Middle East and North Africa Regional studies included Egypt in a working paper covering wages and child labor, and another on youth employment a few years later. The Bank produced a report entitled "Toward a More Effective Social Policy—Subsidies and Social Safety Net" (World Bank 2005d). It also undertook a program of reimbursable TA to pension reform. As of the end of the review period, the Bank has offered to follow up with additional assistance on subsidies and pensions, via both AAA and lending.

The SFD II project (1996) closed well into the review period and was followed by the SFD III project (1999). There has been no new Bank lending to SFD since, and the government dropped a proposed fourth project (Community and Local Development) in late fiscal 2007 at an advanced stage of processing. Besides SFD, a Social Protection Initiatives Learning and Innovation Loan (1999) tested programs for children with disabilities and youth at risk.

Outcomes

Food subsidies remained unchanged through the first half of the review period (years of slowing economic growth) despite an increasing poverty headcount. Subsidies were broadened to eight items, but included new less subsidized bread varieties and rose to 1.5–2.0 percent of GDP in 2004 to mitigate the impact of a substantial devaluation. The Ministry of Social Affairs transfers have remained very modest. Bank analysis demonstrated that a high proportion of existing subsidies benefit the nonpoor.

The Bank had little or no apparent impact on subsidies in the first half of the review period. However, a Luxor workshop in February 2005 marked a turning point. It brought Mr. Wolfensohn—then president of the World Bank Group—and the Bank team, with top international practitioners, together with the Prime Minster and Cabinet to discuss social safety net and subsidy reform. This high-level attention and Bank convening power inspired the government to request further Bank assistance, leading to the production of "Toward a More Effective Social Policy—Subsidies and Social Safety Net" (World Bank 2005d). This report covered both macroeconomic and microeconomic (distributional and efficiency) aspects and gave the government well-argued and nuanced recommendations to increase coverage of the poor, increase cash transfers, and selectively reduce or eliminate those existing food subsidies enjoyed mainly by the nonpoor. Recent and ongoing work is following up on possible reforms, including conditional cash transfers. However, given its political caution and rising international grain prices, the government is likely to proceed slowly. On pension reform, the Bank delivered several policy notes, notes on the institutional reform and implementation strategy, and a draft pension law for a new multipillar pension system.

SFD has implemented very large numbers of worthwhile public works and community development projects. From 1997 to 2006, these projects included more than 1,300 kilometers of rural roads constructed or upgraded and more than 4,000 kilometers of potable water networks; 17,000 classrooms established and nearly 50,000 teachers trained for literacy classes; about 500 health clinics established, rehabilitated, and/or equipped and nearly 15,000 health personnel trained; capacity building for 2,000 nongovernmental organizations; and the creation of some 50,000 permanent jobs.

SFD has also built up important experience, capacities, systems, and relationships. Its donor coordination arrangements were identified as a best practice in IEG's review of the effectiveness of social funds (IEG 2002). However, with the exception of job creation through its Small Enterprise Development Organization (about 350,000 permanent jobs in 1997–2001 alone), the scale of SFD operations was limited in relation to the national problems. SFD has missed important opportunities by not targeting the poor, limited consultation with local governments and communities, and limited monitoring and evaluation. SFD's sustainability was always an issue, and so was its relation to the government centrally and locally. As is usual with social funds, SFD operations created decision-making, operating, and financial systems parallel to or instead of those of local governments, which was acceptable only temporarily until the latter could take over.

Assessing the Bank's contribution

The Bank carried out good analytical work on subsidies and social safety nets that is now being used in designing reforms. Also, it made a considerable contribution to the institutional capacity of the SFD, which is available for transfer to local governments. However, institutional development has otherwise been negligible, the risk to development outcomes is high, and there has been no Bank lending in this area since fiscal 1999. The prospects for achievement of the 2005 CAS indicators in this area by mid-2009 are highly uncertain, especially on a reduction of the ratio of subsidies to GDP, including through better targeting of subsidies, on institutional development, and on employment. On employment, the Bank has not financed the Small Enterprise Development Organization's employment creation program, as other financing was adequate, and the government has declined its proposal for continued support to SFD's remaining programs.

Poverty Reduction

Background

Poverty in Egypt began to be documented effectively starting in the mid-1990s. A 1995–96 household survey showed 2.0 percent of the population in extreme poverty (meeting minimum food needs only) within a poverty rate (headcount) of 19.4 percent. Poverty was shallow at 3.4 percent, but with 32 percent of the population in near poverty there was widespread and serious vulnerability to shocks. The poverty rate in metropolitan and other urban areas varied between 8.3 and 13.1 percent, and rural areas were much worse off: 21.5 percent were poor in rural Lower Egypt and 29.3 percent in rural Upper Egypt.

The Bank's objectives and program

The 1997 CAS focused on analytical work on poverty to help improve the social safety net. In the 2001 CAS, the strategy was to focus on filling the major knowledge gaps on the extent and nature of poverty. Operations would address poverty, which was largely rural, via increasing encouragement of community-based development and water/sanitation. In the 2005 CAS, the strategy is to focus on Upper Egypt—both urban and rural—through PER work and through support for social services and infrastructure investments, involving deconcentration of public service delivery, involvement of civil society, and capacity building. The CAS also proposed further investment through SFD.

Just before the review period, a demographic and health survey in 1996 and a household survey in 1995–96 revealed a profile of poverty. This was followed by the government's Egypt Human Development Report 1998–99 and its successors. Bank AAA on poverty was absent during the first half of the review period. Then staff found a way to persuade the government to give the Bank access to the data from the 1999–2000 household budget survey and to work with the Bank.

During the remainder of the review period, the Bank's AAA program on poverty produced four major reports: a poverty assessment (World Bank 2002c), a poverty reduction strategy (World Bank 2004), a report on subsidies and the social safety net (World Bank 2005d), and a poverty assessment update (World Bank 2007a). There was also economic and sector work on rural development in Upper Egypt. Finally, there was a working paper on Egypt and the Millennium Development Goals (World Bank 2005c).

The Bank's lending program had more focus on support to economic growth in general than on either "shared growth" or direct contributions to poverty reduction. What there was of the latter has come through three types of lending: (i) water resource projects, particularly irrigation improvement; (ii) two targeted area development projects (Sohag and Matruh); and (iii) SFD employment generation, mainly in small and medium enterprises. However, new lending in both education and training and in social protection included an emphasis on poorer groups or regions, as did some ongoing health, nutrition, and population lending.

Outcomes

Egypt has made some progress in poverty reduction during the review period, but it has been disappointing overall, as shown in table 5.4. The rate of progress in poverty reduction is determined overwhelmingly by Egypt's macroeconomic growth cycles. The CAE review period covers three experiences. The poverty headcount fell from 19.4 percent to 16.7 percent during rapid economic growth in the second half of the 1990s. It rose again through 2005 to its baseline level during a period of slower economic growth. Finally, with the more rapid economic growth that has occurred through the period 2005–07, it is reasonable to assume that the headcount has fallen again, although data are not yet available.

However, not all poverty measures have moved together. The proportion of the population in extreme poverty has increased steadily—during the whole period—from 2 percent to nearly 4 percent. Within the national figures, the rural headcount has always exceeded the urban one. Upper Egypt has lagged behind Lower Egypt, and both its rural and urban headcounts increased even during the rapid growth of the late 1990s and continued to rise slowly through 2005. Yet overall income inequality (Gini coefficient) has lessened during the review period. Also, on international comparisons, the proportions of the population living on $1 and $2 per

Table 5.4: Poverty Indicators (percent)

	1995	2000	2005
Extreme poverty	2.0	2.9	3.8
Poverty rate	19.4	16.7	19.6
Metropolitan	13.1	5.1	5.7
Rural Upper Egypt	29.3	34.2	39.1
$1/day	7.0	3.3	3.4
$2/day	57.0	43.7	42.8
Gini coefficient	34.5	36.1	32.1

Source: World Bank 2007a.

day have diminished. Although Egypt has a higher poverty rate than the middle-income Middle East and North Africa Region's countries and Turkey, it fares better than richer countries such as the Philippines and Indonesia, and in terms of extreme poverty better than Brazil and Mexico.

The existing social safety nets—especially a subsidy on bread—do lift some of the poor out of poverty, but too few. In contrast, there has been considerable progress in human development aspects of poverty reduction: education and health, nutrition, and population. Actions to increase access to education by disadvantaged groups and to invest more and provide more services in Upper Egypt and in rural areas were carried out in the early part of the period.

Assessing the Bank's contribution

The poverty assessments brought the facts about poverty to the government's and public's attention. They have helped create a system for continuing poverty monitoring. The 2007 update provided the government with poverty maps to use as a basis to geographically target interventions. The poverty work has also provided intellectual input to the government's strategy for poverty reduction that was adopted during the review period. Finally, the analytical work on subsidies and the social safety net have provided the government with the information required to increase and target needed assistance to the poor while limiting the overall fiscal impact.

However, the Bank's lending program has not been devised and implemented with as strong a poverty/shared growth orientation as would have been possible and desirable. Its direct contribution to income poverty reduction through lending, although diverse, has been modest. Its human development lending has had a useful but limited poverty orientation and impact.

Summary

The Bank's assistance strategy was effective in helping Egypt make good progress in implementing a broad range of social programs.

The Bank's program in gender is rated *satisfactory*. Gender efforts have been mainstreamed to a considerable extent in Egypt, notably in the government's five-year plans. In education, gender disparities have been reduced substantially. Women's health and health services have improved substantially during the review period. In the economic sectors, female participation is increasing, though slowly, and obstacles to entrepreneurship are becoming better understood. Gender-disaggregated data are still limited, however. Overall, Bank gender work in Egypt has pioneered in and been the model for the Middle East and North Africa Region.

The Bank's assistance to education and training is assessed as *satisfactory*. Access has increased to universal primary education and near-universal junior secondary education (middle school); the gender gap has been eliminated at the primary level and is now limited at the junior secondary level. These achievements, along with the maintenance of a lending relationship across all subsectors and throughout the period despite IDA graduation, outweigh the record on other CAS indicators. There has been only partial achievement of the quality objectives of curriculum reform, employer input, and increased learning achievement. Reforms of university governance, autonomy, and financing and improvement of education sector policy making and monitoring and evaluation have not been achieved so far.

The Bank's assistance to health, nutrition, and population is assessed as *moderately satisfactory*. Population/family planning and communicable disease control indicators have been achieved. A new family health service model of primary care has been demonstrated successfully, but participation by the poor and financing for the scheme through health insurance have not yet been achieved on a sustainable basis. Partly as a result, there has been no new Bank lending in health, nutrition, and population during the review period.

The Bank program on subsidies, social safety nets, and social infrastructure is assessed as *mod-*

Table 5.5: Pillar 3: Summary Outcome Rating

Objectives	Outcome rating
Human development and poverty reduction	**Moderately satisfactory**
Gender	Satisfactory
Education and training	Satisfactory
Health, nutrition, and population	Moderately satisfactory
Subsidies, social safety nets, and social infrastructure	Moderately unsatisfactory

Source: IEG.

erately unsatisfactory. The CAS indicators are nearly all for 2009 and had not been achieved as of mid-2007. The Bank has carried out good analytical work on subsidies and social safety nets, which is being used in designing reforms. Also, it has made a considerable contribution to the institutional capacity of the SFD, which is available for transfer to local governments. However, institutional development has otherwise been negligible, the risk to development outcomes is high, and there has been no Bank lending in this area since fiscal 1999.

Poverty analysis began and was carried out successfully through the review period, with three major reports. The Bank's technical expertise on social and equity issues supported a comprehensive poverty reduction strategy designed by the Ministry of Labor during the period, including the safety net issue. Actions to increase access to education by disadvantaged groups, and to invest more and provide more services in Upper Egypt and in rural areas, were carried out at least in the early part of the period.

Table 5.5 summarizes the outcome ratings of the Bank's program in individual themes and sectors and provides an overall outcome rating. Lessons learned and recommendations for future Bank assistance are in chapter 6.

The World Bank is helping Egypt build institutions and capacity to improve the investment climate, increase job opportunities, and promote the flow of foreign direct investment. These reforms will stabilize the Egyptian economy and facilitate its integration regionally and globally in a sustainable manner. © Christophe Boisvieux/Corbis.

Chapter 6

Egypt has made solid progress over the review period with Bank support, focusing on equity and social policy while maintaining the pace of implementation of pro-growth measures. Photo courtesy of Victor Orozco, World Bank Group.

Conclusions, Lessons, and Recommendations

Overall Assessment

The Bank's assistance strategy was relevant, focusing initially on water resources management and the social sectors, then on strengthening the base for higher and sustained growth, in particular through helping to improve the investment climate, reform the financial sector, and improve infrastructure. The Bank's assistance program achieved acceptable progress toward most of its relevant objectives.

Therefore, the overall outcome of the Bank assistance program is rated *moderately satisfactory* (see table 6.1). Although the Bank's financial support was modest (relatively little lending), its analytic work and policy advice resulted in significant contributions to reforms and policy changes across many sectors and subsectors.

Bank assistance helped achieve *good outcomes in its first pillar, promoting higher, more sustainable growth through structural reforms,* although there were two distinct subperiods. During the first half of the period under review (fiscal 1999–2003), the Egyptian economy was affected by external shocks: the emerging market crisis, the terrorist incident in Luxor and the sharp decline in oil prices in 1998, and the slowdown in economic structural reform efforts. This was followed by the global economic fallout from the September 11, 2001, attacks. The situation was further aggravated by the war in Iraq, the consequent uncertain political conditions in the Region, and the sluggish global environment. Real GDP growth declined from 6.1 percent in 1999 to 3.5 percent in 2001. Economic activity in 2002–03 remained constrained by a shortage of foreign currency, high real interest rates, and a depressed Regional and global environment.

Macroeconomic indicators improved in the second subperiod (fiscal 2004–07). The government improved its macroeconomic management, lowered trade tariffs, and renewed efforts to promote the private sector. Tax reform in 2005 lowered personal income and corporate tax rates, widened the tax base, and improved tax and customs administration. Some progress has been made in reducing public expenditures as a share of GDP.

These fiscal measures led to a reduction in fiscal deficits, although they are still high to assure macroeconomic stability. Fiscal consolidation has remained a priority. Financial sector reform has so far been highly satisfactory. The government's reforms in this area have been based on the joint

Bank–IMF financial sector assessment and were supported by a Bank loan, which was supplemented by other donor aid (USAID and AfDB). Less progress was achieved, however, in improving governance, although there were specific achievements in selected areas, such as PFM, especially in tax reform.

Trade increased following an exchange rate correction in 2003 and continued to do so after subsequent tariff reductions from 2004 to 2007. Business climate improvements have augmented the benefits of trade reforms. The Bank's ICAs helped shape the reform program for private sector development. Foreign direct investment and private sector investments have increased over the past few years. Employment grew at 4.6 percent per year during the CAE period. Growth rates accelerated to 7 percent per annum in 2006 and 2007, up from 3 percent in the pre-reform years. The outcome of the first pillar is rated *moderately satisfactory*.

Under the second pillar, *improving water resources management, infrastructure, and environmental management*, outcomes have been mostly satisfactory. For three decades the Bank has been Egypt's principal development partner in irrigation and water management as well as in community-based rural development. Bank-financed irrigation projects introduced new technologies and organizations, which eliminated the prior chaos, wastage, and inequity among farmers. Agricultural productivity improved for major crops, such as cotton, wheat, rice, and broad beans; it ranged from 10 to 20 percent between 1998–99 and 2004–05. In the infrastructure sectors, airport capacity has increased; installed power generation did as well, and chronic power shortages have been avoided. Telephone services have been expanded dramatically. Some progress has been made in improving air and water quality. The outcome of the Bank's program for the second pillar is rated *satisfactory*.

The outcomes of Bank assistance in the third pillar, *human development and poverty reduction*, have been *moderately satisfactory*. Gender has been mainstreamed to a considerable extent in Egypt, notably in the government's five-year plans. Egypt has made sustained progress toward the Millennium Development Goals for education, infant and child mortality, maternal mortality, and access to safe water and sanitation. In particular, infant and under-five mortality rates have declined to almost one-quarter of their 1990 levels, and primary and secondary enrollments have increased substantially. Many social indicators are better in Egypt than in countries with comparable income levels.

Progress in poverty reduction is determined primarily by Egypt's macroeconomic growth cycles and has been disappointing overall, with little reduction in the headcount over the review period. Upper Egypt continues to lag. Food subsidies offer some relief but reach too few of the poor and are not well targeted. The Bank's poverty analysis work has been extensive and appreciated. However, its lending program has, in general, focused on economic growth more than on poverty reduction and shared growth.

Table 6.1: Overall Outcome Ratings

Objectives	Outcomes
Overall	**Moderately satisfactory**
Promoting higher, more sustainable growth through structural reforms	Moderately satisfactory
Improving water resources, infrastructure, and environment	Satisfactory
Human development and poverty reduction	Moderately satisfactory

Source: IEG.

Institutional Development Impact

Institutional development impact is rated substantial. Much of the enabling framework of legislation and institutions was put in place, particularly during the second half of the review period. The tax policy framework and tax administration have been reformed. Cash and debt management were streamlined by the consolidation of major government accounts into a TSA. The TSA eliminated and replaced some 5,000 accounts, improving the budget accounting system drastically. A new customs law and its implementing regulations have simplified the customs regime and changed it from an institution of control compliance to one that is trade-facilitating in nature.

Banking reforms included a new banking law, the exit of several weak banks, large-scale financial restructuring involving the buy-out and provisioning of nonperforming loans, and the privatization of one major state bank, Bank of Alexandria. The Central Bank of Egypt has become a modern central bank, focused on monetary policy and the regulation and supervision of the banking system.

In water resources management, there has been significant strengthening of institutions, including the Egyptian Authority for Public Drainage Projects and water user associations. The implementation of an integrated water resources plan is under way. The role of the regulatory body was strengthened in a new telecommunications law in early 2003, which established the National Telecommunications Regulatory Agency.

The Bank has been helping institutional development in the transportation and energy sectors as well. The NCW became the focal point for the government's gender efforts. In education and health, the legal framework and core institutions have strengthened in recent years. A new Ministry of Social Solidarity was created to develop and implement reforms of the social safety net.

Risks to Development Outcomes

The government has been stable for several decades and has proved able to carry out substantial changes in economic policies, including a comprehensive structural adjustment program in 1991 that lasted for a number of years, without undue social unrest or political upheaval. There is thus reason to think that the government will be able to maintain the current reform momentum.

In addition, support for current reforms is widespread across key ministries and includes a shared vision and a cohesive relationship between the Prime Minister and reform-minded ministries. These include the Ministries of Finance, Investment, Trade and Industry, and Transportation.

The impetus for the current set of reforms came from a desire for more rapid growth, rather than as a result of crisis. Based on experience in other countries, this is a positive indicator, as crisis-generated reforms often lose momentum and political support once the crisis has passed.

Finally, this reform program has been home grown, the result of government initiative, and has included effective public communications. External partners such as the Bank and the IMF have had a low profile in the process, which reduces the potential for resistance from the public to the reforms.

However, important areas of reform continue to move slowly or have not yet been adequately addressed, and these areas could undermine the progress made. For example, high energy subsidies, the absence of significant civil service reform, and the remaining loss-making public enterprises could undermine fiscal discipline. In addition, public investment remains inadequate (on a downward path as a percent of GDP), which could inhibit private investment and growth.

The government has, correctly, targeted reforms that have had the least direct negative impact on people in the short run. The next round of reforms, such as reducing energy subsidies, retrenchment of public sector salaries, civil service reform, or further enterprise privatization, would be more far reaching, more unpopular, and therefore more politically difficult. A vocal media opposition has developed against the privatization program, for example, especially the sale of public assets to foreign investors. The media could both reflect and stir up further resentment against reforms, which in turn could cause the government to halt or slow the process.

Finally, it is not clear that increased capacity and improved social services, particularly in health, can be sustained without further support. For example, the central department responsible for disease surveillance remains weak; family planning services could be affected if the declining support from USAID is not replaced; and the SFD's network of community health workers may not be able to continue to function without additional funding. The new family health model has not yet provided access for the poor or financial sustainability, and the new health insurance program could face opposition, as did its predecessor.

Going forward, there are three types of risk to Egypt's otherwise positive outlook. The first is continued fiscal fragility—despite tax reforms, the consolidation of major government accounts into single treasury account, and reduction of domestic debt. Fiscal discipline needs to continue, with the government aiming to cut the budget deficit to 3 percent of GDP by 2010–11. Subsidy reform has already proven difficult as protests grow in response to rising food prices.

Second, there is a risk of regional instability, although conflict in neighboring West Bank and Gaza and Iraq has not caused instability in Egypt. But further deterioration of regional stability and likely global recession may affect at least tourism revenues, workers' remittances, and Suez Canal revenues.

Third, dramatic increases in international food prices have posed difficult choices for the government. The government sought to address potential discontent in several ways, although they have been fiscally costly. It separated the production and sale of subsidized bread—the main element in the Egyptian diet—to reduce corruption; it also reduced customs duties on key staples, including rice, wheat, cooking oil, and dairy products, and imposed a ban on rice exports. Finally, it is maintaining the retail price of subsidized bread and drastically expanding the numbers of citizens who are eligible for food subsidies.

Main Findings and Lessons

The Bank did a good job of assessing Egypt's development needs—its strategic objectives were relevant. The Bank's assistance strategies also recognized from the start that a major part of the Bank Group's contribution to Egypt's development would come from nonlending services that respond to government requests for analytical assistance and policy advice. In many sectors, the Bank's policy advice was sound and consistent and remained valid over the course of the CAE period. The Bank has managed to influence policy over the years, even in areas where there was no lending (trade reform and private sector development) or where lending was picked up by other donors (telecommunications). In addition, Bank strategies became more focused in the second half of the review period. For example, high case triggers and lending are directed uniquely to financial sector reforms in the 2005 CAS.

The availability of cheaper sources of finance from other donors, the reluctance of the government to increase foreign debt above its 1997 level, and the requirement that new loans should have a grant element of at least 40 percent all created limited interest in Bank finance, especially after Egypt graduated from IDA in 1999. In this environment, the Bank focused on cleaning up the portfolio in 2002–04, relinquished unused resources, even on IDA terms, and tightened quality standards. These changes not only improved lending performance (dropped and problem projects, project outcome ratings) but also freed resources for economic and sector work.

Analytical work, even if not used immediately, turned out to be useful, partly for creating awareness of the issues and partly for defining priority reforms once the government decided to act. It also gave credibility to the Bank, in that once a more reform-minded government took office, Bank inputs were valued. This was most evident in the Bank's work on the financial sector (joint Bank–International Monetary Fund–FSAP) and trade regime.

The experience over the past 10 years in Egypt highlights once again the futility of pushing for reforms and for policy-based lending in support of those reforms with an unwilling or uninterested government. In the first part of the review period, the Bank tried and failed to agree on policy-based loans; in the second part of the period, following a change in government and the arrival of a reform-minded Cabinet, the Bank was able to support a series of reforms across a number of sectors, through a combination of policy dialogue, nonlending TA, and a policy-based loan. The change in the government's approach to reforms made all the difference.

The Bank's experience in the Airports Development Project is more complicated to assess. On one hand, it was only indirectly linked to poverty reduction and arguably not the most exemplary reflection of the Bank's mandate to prioritize poverty reduction in its support to client countries. On the other hand, one of the main factors in the creation of a close working partnership with the government in a number of infrastructure sectors during this period was the Bank's ability to respond with speed and high quality to the government's request for support on the airports project, thus countering the Bank's reputation as slow and overly bureaucratic. The positive experience gave the Bank greater credibility, which subsequently extended to policy discussions, such as advice on liberalization of civil aviation, regulation, and privatization, as well as to project preparation and implementation.

A series of education and training projects with Bank financing from 1997 to 2005 has made a substantial contribution to the sector's progress. The main factors contributing to this progress were Egypt's commitment to the sector, trust, unusual continuity of senior Egyptian personnel and the Bank team, the quality of the project contents (particularly the Primary and Higher Education Enhancement Projects), and attractive cofinancing packages.

In the area of social infrastructure, the Bank's lending and institutional assistance to the SFD contributed to the creation of some permanent and much temporary employment, useful local infrastructure (rural roads, potable water networks, and health clinics), and training. However, the Bank failed to press earlier and harder for pro-poor targeting by SFD, which had a limited impact on poverty.

Recommendations

Future Bank strategy should reflect Egypt's middle-income status by including a flexible lending program and emphasis on knowledge services, including reimbursable TA. The Bank should also build on the recent success of reform efforts in the financial sector and on its role as financier and advisor in infrastructure sectors (transportation, energy, and telecommunications). The main recommendations for strengthening what has recently been a successful partnership strategy include—

- Enhancing the assistance program's focus on the persistent issue of *poverty and income disparities,* with a view to identifying direct and indirect interventions that could reduce income disparities in particular, including improving the efficiency and targeting of social safety nets through the introduction of a program of conditional cash transfers. This would strengthen the social dimension of the assistance strategy and ensure that a greater share of reform benefits would go to the poor. Much of the knowledge base on poverty—including the poverty mapping as part of the latest poverty update of 2007—and subsidy reform has already been built. In addition, lending, particularly but not exclusively for human development, should be more focused on Upper

Egypt, with a view to decreasing disparities in living standards between Lower and Upper Egypt. Lessons on implementing a comprehensive and broad conditional cash transfers program could be adapted to the Egyptian setting not only from Mexico but also other middle-income countries such as Brazil and Turkey.

- Strengthening analytic work by placing greater emphasis than in the past on macroeconomic analysis, water resources development, infrastructure, and Upper Egypt and improving the engagement of stakeholders around the findings and recommendations.

Financial sector and PSG

- Continue lending support to financial sector reforms, which are still incomplete. Specifically, complete banking reform, including specialized banks, supervisory framework, capital markets (corporate bonds, enhancing the Capital Market Authority's governance capacity and revitalizing primary markets), and nonbanking financial institutions (the insurance and pension fund sector).
- Continue promoting improvements to systems that indirectly combat corruption (PFM, simplification of taxation and business procedures, and information acts).

Water resources, infrastructure, and environment sectors

- *Agriculture*: Strengthen dialogue with the agriculture ministry with an aim to enhance linkage between agricultural policies and water management.
- *Infrastructure*: Assist Egypt in developing its infrastructure strategy and move beyond capital investments. Focus on policy and institutional reforms in energy and transportation.
- *Environment:* Improve strategic focus of an assistance strategy by building on the recent analytical work (Country Environmental Assessment) and agree with the government on a program of support with other donors.

Human development

- *Health:* Focus on the family health model and on reforming health financing.
- *Education:* Narrow the focus to one or a small number of larger loans for improving the quality of secondary and higher education and to policy and institutional reforms.

Appendixes

Egypt's programs during the review period focused on enhancing the provision of public services, such as infrastructure services including power, communications, and transportation. Photo by Ray Witlin, courtesy of the World Bank Photo Library.

APPENDIX A: STATISTICAL SUPPLEMENT

Table A.1: Egypt at a Glance

	Egypt, Arab Rep. of	M. East & North Africa	Lower-middle-income
POVERTY and SOCIAL			
2006			
Population, mid-year (*millions*)	75.5	313	3,437
GNI per capita (*Atlas method, $*)	1,580	2,794	1,887
GNI (*Atlas method, $ billions*)	119.4	876	6,485
Average annual growth, 2001–07			
Population (%)	1.8	1.8	1.1
Labor force (%)	2.8	3.6	1.5
Most recent estimate (latest year available, 2001–07)			
Poverty (*% of population below national poverty line*)	—	—	—
Urban population (*% of total population*)	43	57	42
Life expectancy at birth (*years*)	71	70	69
Infant mortality (per 1,000 live births)	29	34	41
Child malnutrition (*% of children under 5*)	5	..	25
Access to an improved water source (*% of population*)	98	89	88
Literacy (*% of population age 15+*)	71	73	89
Gross primary enrollment (*% of school-age population*)	105	105	111
Male	107	108	112
Female	102	103	109

Development diamond[a]

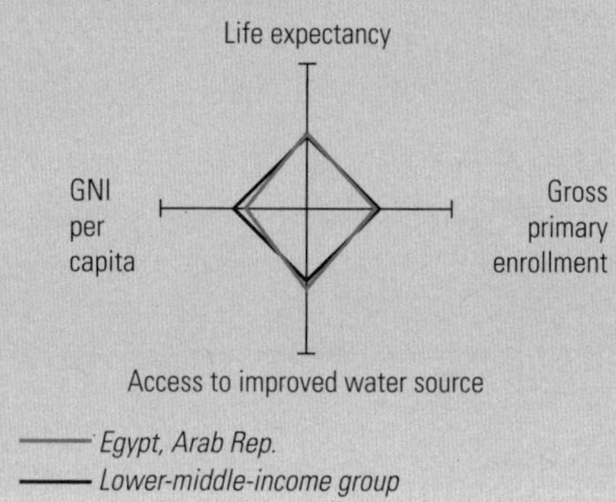

KEY ECONOMIC RATIOS and LONG-TERM TRENDS

	1987	1997	2006	2007
GDP (*$ billions*)	40.5	78.4	107.5	128.1
Gross capital formation/GDP	26.1	17.6	18.7	21.9
Exports of goods and services/GDP	12.6	18.8	29.9	31.3
Gross domestic savings/GDP	15.9	11.5	17.1	14.0
Gross national savings/GDP	19.1	17.3	22.0	24.3
Current account balance/GDP	–2.3	0.2	1.6	2.1
Interest payments/GDP	1.2	1.0	0.6	—
Total debt/GDP	109.0	38.4	27.3	—
Total debt service/exports	17.9	10.0	5.4	—
Present value of debt/GDP	—	—	24.0	—
Present value of debt/exports	—	—	63.1	—

	1987–97	1997–07	2006	2007	2007–11
(*average annual growth*)					
GDP	4.1	4.5	6.8	7.1	6.8
GDP per capita	2.0	2.6	4.9	5.2	5.7
Exports of goods and services	6.3	9.5	21.3	14.2	19.6

Economic ratios[a]

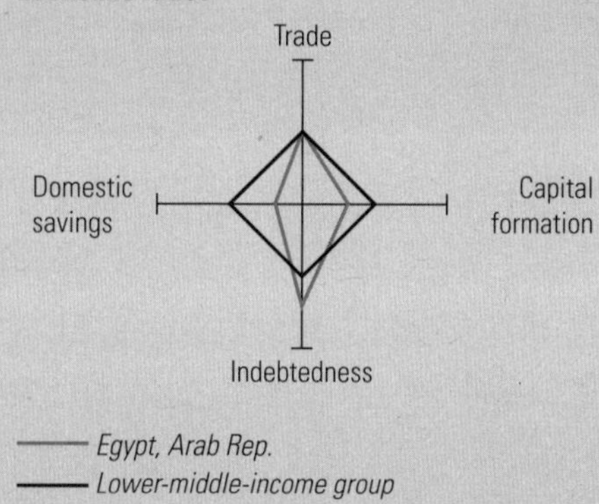

STRUCTURE of the ECONOMY

	1987	1997	2006	2007
(*% of GDP*)				
Agriculture	20.5	17.0	14.1	13.0
Industry	27.1	31.2	38.4	35.5
Manufacturing	16.5	17.6	16.6	15.8
Services	52.4	51.8	47.5	51.5
Household final consumption expenditure	69.9	77.2	70.6	74.8
General gov't final consumption expenditure	14.3	11.3	12.3	11.2
Imports of goods and services	22.8	24.9	31.6	39.2

Growth of capital and GDP (%)

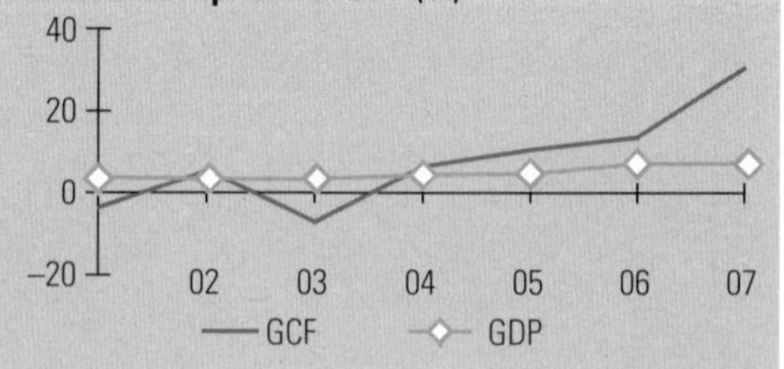

Table A.1: Egypt at a Glance

	1987–97	1997–07	2006	2007
(average annual growth)				
Agriculture	2.8	3.4	3.2	3.7
Industry	6.3	4.3	9.8	8.0
Manufacturing	5.3	4.9	5.9	7.6
Services	2.7	4.8	6.1	5.3
Household final consumption expenditure	4.7	3.4	5.2	6.5
General gov't final consumption expenditure	2.3	4.1	3.1	20.0
Gross capital formation	–1.2	4.7	13.3	30.1
Imports of goods and services	2.5	6.7	21.8	27.8

Growth of exports and imports (%)

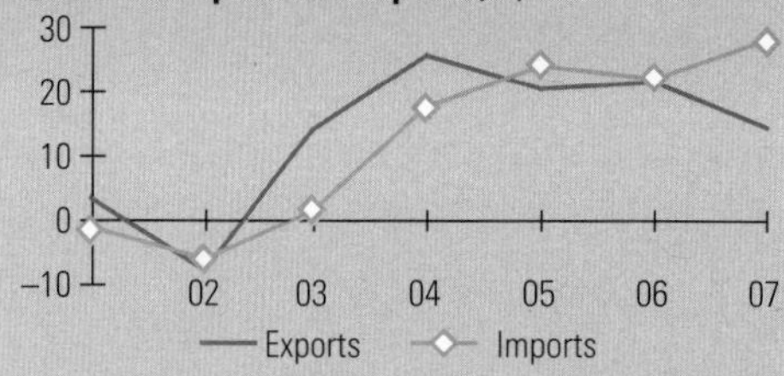

PRICES and GOVERNMENT FINANCE

	1987	1997	2006	2007
Domestic prices				
(% change)				
Consumer prices	—	6.2	4.2	10.4
Implicit GDP deflator	31.1	9.9	7.4	10.5
Government finance				
(% of GDP, includes current grants)				
Current revenue	20.3	22.8	27.3	25.3
Current budget balance	20.3	22.8	27.4	0.3
Overall surplus/deficit	26.2	24.3	28.5	–8.3

Inflation (%)

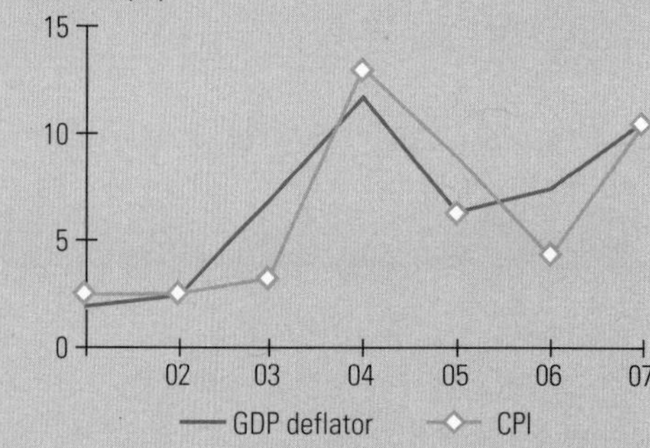

TRADE

	1987	1997	2006	2007
($ millions)				
Total exports (fob)	2,264	5,345	18,455	21,336
Cotton	458	2,578	10,407	11,038
Other agriculture	343	107	146	182
Manufactures	665	1,302	5,172	5,947
Total imports (cif)	7,323	15,565	30,441	37,469
Food	2,338	2,885	1,921	2,159
Fuel and energy	884	1,909	5,443	5,928
Capital goods	1,764	4,114	7,888	12,030
Export price index (*2000=100*)	87	126	150	157
Import price index (*2000=100*)	86	116	135	138
Terms of trade (*2000=100*)	101	108	111	113

Export and import levels ($ mill.)

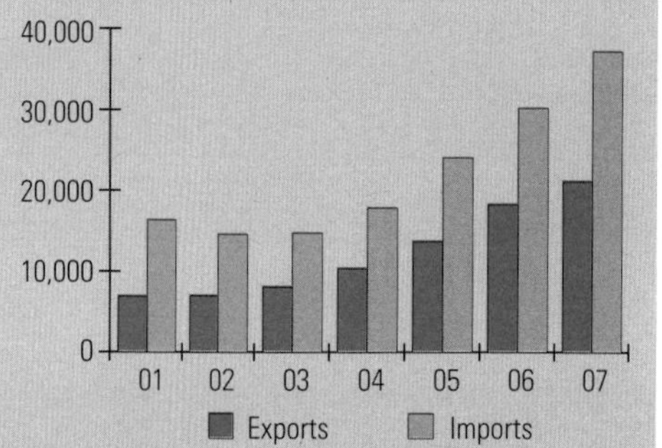

BALANCE of PAYMENTS

	1987	1997	2006	2007
($ millions)				
Exports of goods and services	5,667	14,534	33,891	40,008
Imports of goods and services	9,468	19,528	38,217	50,121
Resource balance	–3,801	–4,994	–4,326	–10,114
Net income	–480	967	531	940
Net current transfers	3,356	4,145	5,547	11,915
Current account balance	–924	119	1,752	2,741
Financing items (net)	106	1,793	1,502	3,940
Changes in net reserves	819	–1,912	–3,253	–6,681
Memo:				
Reserves including gold (*$ millions*)	—	—	26,660	30,320
Conversion rate (*DEC, local/$*)	1.3	3.4	5.7	5.7

Current account balance to GDP (%)

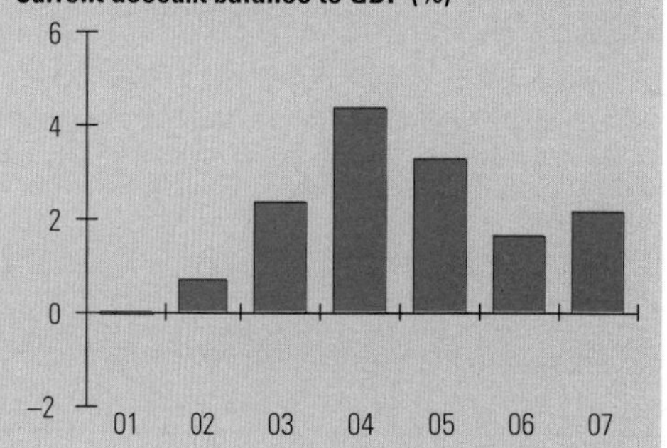

(*Continued on the following page*)

Table A.1: Egypt at a Glance (*continued*)

EXTERNAL DEBT and RESOURCE FLOWS	1987	1997	2006	2007
(*$ millions*)				
Total debt outstanding and disbursed	44,147	30,102	29,339	—
IBRD	1,703	869	544	1,181
IDA	892	1,206	1,481	1,490
Total debt service	1,661	1,985	2,201	—
IBRD	244	297	93	144
IDA	10	24	53	58
Composition of net resource flows				
Official grants	560	1,028	639	—
Official creditors		753	−10	−1,040
Private creditors	574	−37	−250	—
Foreign direct investment (net inflows)	948	891	10,043	—
Portfolio equity (net inflows)	0	515	502	—
World Bank program				
Commitments	0	75	817	0
Disbursements	163	260	164	737
Principal repayments	125	241	108	144
Net flows	38	19	56	593
Interest payments	129	80	39	58
Net transfers	−91	−61	18	535

Composition of 2006 debt ($ mill.)

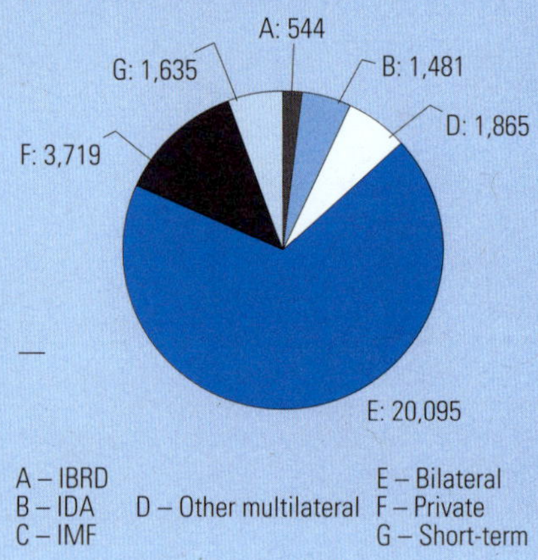

Source: Development Economics LDB database. This table was prepared by country unit staff; figures may differ from other World Bank published data.

Note: 2006 data are preliminary estimates. cif = cost, insurance, and freight; DEC = Development Economics and Chief Economist; fob = free on board; GDP = gross domestic product; GNI = gross national income; IBRD = International Bank for Reconstruction and Development; IDA = International Development Association; IMF = International Monetary Fund.

a. The diamonds show four key indicators in the country (in bold) compared with its income-group average. If data are missing, the diamond will be incomplete.

Table A.2: Social Indicators, 1996–2005/06

Indicators	Fiscal Year 1997	1998	1999	2000	2001	2002	2003	2004	2005	2006	Egypt, Arab Rep. of (1997–2006 average)	Yemen, Rep.	Morocco	Syrian Arab Rep.	Algeria	Tunisia	Indonesia	Turkey	Lower middle-income	Middle East and North Africa
Growth and inflation																				
GDP growth (annual %)[a]	5.5	4.0	6.1	5.4	3.5	3.2	3.1	4.2	4.5	6.8	4.6	4.5	3.5	3.3	3.9	4.9	2.6	4.2	6.6	4.1
GDP per capita growth (annual %)	3.5	2.1	4.1	3.4	1.6	1.2	1.2	2.2	2.5	4.9	2.7	1.3	2.2	0.7	2.4	3.7	1.3	2.7	5.5	2.2
GNI per capita, PPP (current international $)	3,080	3,200	3,380	3,560	3,700	3,820	3,900	4,090	4,310	4,690	3,773	797	3,898	3,310	5,617	6,595	3,117	6,976	4,757	5,146
GNI per capita, Atlas method (current $)	1,150	1,220	1,340	1,450	1,460	1,400	1,310	1,250	1,250	1,350	1,318	489	1,386	1,129	1,970	2,313	923	3,360	1,306	1,836
Inflation, consumer prices (annual %)[a]	4.6	3.9	3.1	2.8	2.4	2.4	3.2	8.1	8.8	4.2	4.8	8.1	1.7	–0.4	3.0	3.0	14.9	44.1	—	—
Composition of GDP (%)																				
Agriculture, value added	17.0	17.1	17.3	16.7	16.6	16.5	16.7	15.2	14.9	—	16.4	14.3	15.7	26.6	10.3	12.1	15.8	14.2	13.9	12.8
Industry, value added	31.2	30.9	30.9	33.1	33.3	33.2	34.5	36.9	36.1	—	33.3	40.9	30.9	32.6	53.8	28.6	44.7	24.3	42.1	41.0
Services, value added	51.8	52.0	51.8	50.1	50.1	50.3	48.8	48.0	49.0	—	50.2	44.8	53.4	40.8	35.9	59.3	39.4	61.5	44.0	46.1
External accounts																				
Exports of goods and services (% of GDP)	18.8	16.2	15.1	16.2	17.5	18.3	21.8	28.2	30.3	31.3	21.4	36.3	32.4	33.7	35.4	46.0	35.4	27.1	31.6	28.5
Imports of goods and services (% of GDP)	24.9	25.7	23.3	22.8	22.3	22.7	24.4	29.6	32.6	33.7	26.2	41.0	37.6	30.8	23.2	49.0	29.4	31.2	30.4	29.3
Current account balance (% of GDP)	–0.9	–3.0	–1.8	–1.0	–0.4	0.7	4.5	5.0	2.3	—	0.6	4.4	1.6	2.2	—	–3.0	2.6	–2.2	—	—
Total reserves in months of imports	10.5	10.2	8.0	6.9	7.5	8.3	8.6	6.6	7.3	—	8.2	8.2	6.9	—	—	2.6	5.3	4.7	8.6	—
External debt (% of GNI)	38.1	37.8	33.8	28.9	29.8	33.8	37.8	38.5	38.3	—	35.2	62.0	54.9	108.1	45.2	66.7	84.8	57.5	33.4	38.6
Gross fixed capital formation (% of GDP)	17.9	21.3	20.8	18.9	17.7	17.8	16.3	16.4	17.9	18.7	18.4	22.6	23.5	20.5	23.7	24.4	21.7	20.0	29.6	22.6
Fiscal accounts (% of GDP)																				
Current revenue, including current grants[b]	22.9	22.2	21.9	27.9	27.2	23.3	24.3	23.7	23.0	27.3	24.4	32.8	23.6	29.7	36.1	24.2	17.7	26.5	—	—
Expenditure, total[b]	23.7	23.2	26.0	29.6	29.9	33.3	33.8	32.9	31.6	36.5	30.0	34.1	27.6	30.8	30.3	27.5	24.8	—	—	—
Overall budget balance, including grants[b]	–0.9	–1.0	–4.1	–1.8	–2.7	-10.0	–9.4	–9.1	-8.6	–9.2	–5.7	–1.2	–3.3	–1.1	5.7	–3.3	–2.0	–9.2	–2.6	—
Social indicators																				
Health																				
Immunization, DPT (% of children age 12–23 months)	88.0	91.0	94.0	98.0	99.0	97.0	98.0	97.0	98.0	—	95.6	71.3	94.4	96.1	88.9	96.7	72.4	81.4	84.4	91.4
Improved water source (% of population with access)	—	—	—	97.0	—	—	—	98.0	—	—	97.5	68.0	80.0	90.5	87.0	91.5	76.5	94.5	80.3	89.3
Improved sanitation facilities (% of population with access)	—	—	—	65.0	—	—	—	70.0	—	—	67.5	41.0	71.0	87.0	91.5	84.0	53.5	87.5	54.5	75.9
Life expectancy at birth, total (years)	67.6	—	—	68.8	—	69.6	—	—	70.5	—	69.1	59.8	69.1	72.8	70.5	72.7	66.2	70.2	69.4	68.4
Mortality rate, infant (per 1,000 live births)	—	—	—	40.0	—	—	—	—	28.0	—	34.0	78.5	40.5	15.7	35.5	22.5	32.0	31.8	34.4	46.0
Education																				
School enrollment, preprimary (% gross)	—	—	10.5	11.4	12.3	13.1	13.9	14.4	16.2	—	13.1	0.7	57.4	9.4	4.0	17.6	27.6	7.2	35.6	18.3
School enrollment, primary (% gross)	—	—	101.3	100.5	100.1	100.3	100.5	100.7	100.8	—	100.6	81.8	99.9	113.4	108.9	111.7	115.0	95.8	111.8	99.6
School enrollment, secondary (% gross)	—	—	80.8	83.4	85.9	86.2	86.9	87.1	85.5	—	85.1	45.1	42.9	50.9	79.1	78.0	60.0	79.8	68.1	69.9
Literacy rate, adult total (% of people ages 15 and above)	—	—	—	—	—	—	—	—	71.4	—	71.4	54.1	52.3	81.9	69.9	74.3	90.4	87.4	88.9	73.0
Population																				
Population growth (annual %)	1.9	1.9	1.9	1.9	1.9	1.9	1.9	1.9	1.9	1.8	1.9	3.1	1.3	2.5	1.5	1.1	1.3	1.5	1.0	1.9
Population, total (in million)	63.6	64.8	66.0	67.3	68.6	69.9	71.3	72.6	74.0	75.4	69.3	18.9	29.0	17.5	31.2	9.7	210.6	68.8	2,183.1	287.2
Urban population (% of total)	42.7	42.6	42.6	42.5	42.6	42.6	42.7	42.7	42.8	43.0	42.7	26.0	56.2	50.3	60.8	64.0	43.8	65.5	43.7	56.1

Source: World Development Indicators (September 2007 update) for all indicators excluding those noted.
Note: DPT = diphtheria, pertussis, tetanus; GDP = gross domestic product; GNI = gross national income; PPP = public-private partnership.
a. IMF World Economic Outlook, October 2007.
b. World Bank Middle East and North Africa Region database.

Table A.3: Disbursements of Total Net Official Flows ($ million)

Donor	1999	2000	2001	2002	2003	2004	2005	Total 1999–2005
Multilaterals								
European Commission	217.1	70.3	66.6	50.1	141.3	586.6	1,193.8	2,325.8
International Development Association	13.7	26.3	2.5	20.5	–3.9	36.2	27.8	123.1
International Finance Corporation	23.7	–40.5	29.0	74.1	37.6	1.0	–6.1	118.7
African Development Fund	18.4	9.9	14.2	2.2	12.3	18.1	0.0	75.0
World Food Program	3.6	9.1	1.5	3.2	3.9	3.9	4.1	29.4
International Fund for Agricultural Development	4.5	5.4	–1.0	1.9	1.2	3.3	6.5	21.8
United Nations Transitional Authority	3.8	2.1	3.4	2.7	3.3	2.8	3.5	21.5
United Nations Children's Fund (UNICEF)	3.3	3.2	3.4	2.7	2.5	2.7	2.7	20.4
United Nations High Commissioner for Refugees	4.0	2.5	2.3	2.8	2.7	2.7	1.7	18.7
United Nations Population Fund (UNFPA)	3.2	1.9	3.2	1.1	1.9	2.4	1.8	15.6
United Nations Development Programme	3.9	2.0	1.7	1.5	1.2	1.2	1.2	12.7
Arab Agencies	–0.7	–0.7	1.3	–0.4	0.1	2.6	4.3	6.3
Global Environment Facility	0.6	0.7	0.7	0.1	0.1	0.3	0.5	3.1
Global Fund (GFATM)						0.4	0.9	1.3
African Development Bank	–52.3	–56.8	7.9	–69.9	–41.0	0.4	–88.4	–300.2
International Bank for Reconstruction and Development	–74.2	–80.5	–55.1	–46.6	–48.0	–51.8	19.8	–336.4
Main bilaterals								
United States	900.9	830.2	825.5	1,041.2	637.1	899.9	592.8	5,727.6
France	254.1	240.9	201.5	100.1	100.0	109.2	80.4	1,086.1
Germany	99.0	65.6	99.7	51.6	97.4	88.1	100.4	601.9
Japan	139.1	90.8	95.5	1.8	–3.4	73.9	–71.2	326.4
Denmark	40.1	42.3	25.2	16.1	41.2	24.9	8.3	198.0
Austria	19.9	22.9	21.4	17.6	13.1	12.8	14.6	122.2
Netherlands	16.5	17.3	20.3	17.1	29.3	9.8	7.8	118.0
United Kingdom	5.3	4.1	3.6	12.2	3.5	76.8	6.2	111.6
Canada	12.5	33.6	18.7	6.4	2.8	12.7	7.7	94.4
Spain	2.3	–2.1	8.3	13.5	9.4	19.8	28.5	79.7
Switzerland	10.8	7.0	3.2	4.3	2.8	1.6	9.5	39.2
Australia	4.2	8.7	7.2	4.3	5.2	6.8	1.4	37.8
Italy	18.3	–8.1	2.6	0.8	3.2	18.8	–2.8	32.9
Finland	2.7	3.5	3.7	5.2	4.5	3.9	4.3	27.7
Sweden	1.4	2.6	2.1	2.2	0.0	3.4	2.5	14.2
Greece	0.8	0.7	0.4	0.3	3.6	1.1	3.7	10.7
Korea, Rep. of	0.7	0.2	–0.4	1.0	0.7	1.7	4.4	8.3
Norway	1.2	1.1	0.9	0.6	0.7	0.7	0.6	5.7
Other bilateral donors	1.7				0.0		0.1	1.8
Turkey		0.0		0.0	0.0	0.3	1.2	1.5
Ireland	0.1	0.1	0.0	0.1	0.2	0.0	0.3	0.9
Poland	0.1	0.1	0.0	0.1	0.1	0.1	0.0	0.4

Table A.3: Disbursements of Total Net Official Flows ($ million)

Donor	1999	2000	2001	2002	2003	2004	2005	Total 1999–2005
Czech Republic				0.0	0.1	0.1	0.1	0.3
Luxembourg						0.1	0.1	0.3
New Zealand	0.1	0.0	0.0	0.0	0.0	0.0	0.0	0.1
Slovak Republic				0.0	0.0	0.0		0.1
Portugal			0.0				0.0	0.0
Hungary					0.0	0.0		0.0
Belgium	–1.8	–1.8	–1.9	–4.2	–4.2	–4.3	–4.7	–22.9
Arab countries	70.8	53.1	60.7	28.4	125.7	17.0	23.5	379.2
DAC countries, total	1,527.6	1,359.4	1,337.8	1,290.9	946.3	1,359.9	790.4	8,612.3
DAC EU members, total	458.7	388.0	386.8	232.4	301.1	364.4	249.7	2,381.1
G7, total	1,429.2	1,257.2	1,247.1	1,214.1	840.7	1,279.4	713.4	7,980.9
Non-DAC bilateral donors, total	73.3	53.4	60.4	29.5	126.6	19.1	29.3	391.5
Multilateral, total	172.6	–45.2	81.5	46.0	115.2	612.7	1,174.0	2,156.8
All donors, total	**1,773.4**	**1,367.6**	**1,479.7**	**1,366.5**	**1,188.0**	**1,991.7**	**1,993.7**	**11,160.6**

Source: OECD-DAC online database. Destination of Official Development Assistance and Official Aid-Disbursements as of September 11, 2007.

Note: OFFICIAL DEVELOPMENT ASSISTANCE: Grants or loans to countries and territories on Part I of the DAC List of Aid Recipients (developing countries) that are undertaken by the official sector; with promotion of economic development and welfare as the main objective; at concessional financial terms [if a loan, having a grant element (q.v.) of at least 25 percent]. In addition to financial flows, technical cooperation (q.v.) is included in aid. Grants, loans, and credits for military purposes are excluded. Transfer payments to private individuals (for example, pensions, reparations, or insurance payouts) are in general not counted.

OTHER OFFICIAL FLOWS: Transactions by the official sector with countries on the List of Aid Recipients that do not meet the conditions for eligibility as official development assistance or official aid, either because they are not primarily aimed at development or because they have a grant element of less than 25 percent.

DAC = Development Assistance Committee, Organisation for Economic Cooperation and Development; EU = European Union.

Table A.4a: World Bank Commitments by Sector Board, Fiscal 1993–2007 ($ million)

	Fiscal year														
Sector board	**1993**	**1994**	**1995**	**1996**	**1997**	**1998**	**1999**	**2000**	**2001**	**2002**	**2003**	**2004**	**2005**	**2006**	**2007**
Agriculture and rural development	22.0	121.0	80.0			15.0	445.0	50.0			12.4		120.0		145.0
Education	55.5				75.0		50.0			50.0		5.5	20.0		
Energy and mining				35.0										259.6	
Environment						35.0								20.0	
Financial and private sector development														500.0	37.1
Health, nutrition, and population				17.2		90.0									
Social protection				120.0			55.0								
Transport						2.0						335.0			
Urban development	130.0														
Total commitments	**207.5**	**121.0**	**80.0**	**172.2**	**75.0**	**142.0**	**550.0**	**50.0**	**0.0**	**50.0**	**12.4**	**340.5**	**140.0**	**779.6**	**182.1**

Source: World Bank internal database as of December 20, 2007.

Table A.4b: IBRD/IDA-Approved Projects 1993–2007 (by approval fiscal year)

Project ID	Project name	Approval fiscal year	Sector	IBRD/ IDA amount	Latest DO	Latest IP	Project status	Date, revised closing[c]	IEG outcome	IEG sustainability	IEG ID impact
P045175	Health Sector Reform Program	1998	Health, Nutrition, and Population	90.0	MS	MS	Active	03/31/2009			
P049166	East Delta Agricultural Services Project	1998	Rural	15.0	S	MS	Active	12/31/2008			
P050484	Secondary Education Enhancement Project	1999	Education	50.0	MS	MS	Active	06/30/2010			
P040858	Sohag Rural Development Project	1999	Rural	25.0	S	S	Active	04/30/2008			
P041410	Pumping Stations Rehabilitation III	1999	Rural	120.0	MS	S	Active	08/31/2007			
P045499	National Drainage Project II	2000	Rural	50.0	S	S	Active	12/31/2008			
P056236	Higher Education Enhancement Project	2002	Education	50.0	S	S	Active	12/31/2008			
P049702	Skills Development Project	2004	Education	5.5	S	S	Active	06/30/2010			
P082914	Airports Development Project	2004	Transport	335.0	S	S	Active	06/30/2009			
P082952	Early Childhood Education Enhancement Project	2005	Education	20.0	MU	MU	Active	12/31/2010			
P073977	Integrated Irrigation Improvement and Management Project	2005	Rural	120.0	S	MS	Active	03/31/2014			
P091945	El Tebbin Power Project	2006	Energy and Mining	259.6	S	S	Active	04/30/2011			
P090073	Second Pollution Abatement Project	2006	Environment	20.0	S	S	Active	02/28/2012			
P088877	Financial Sector Reform DPL[a]	2006	Financial	500.0	HS	HS	Active	06/30/2007			
P093470	Mortgage Finance Project	2007	Financial	37.1	S	S	Active	07/31/2011			
P087970	West Delta Water Conservation and Irrigation Rehabilitation Project	2007	Agriculture and Rural Development	145.0	S	S	Active	06/30/2011			
P005161	Basic Education Improvement Project	1993	Education	55.5	S	S	Closed	12/31/2003	MS	Likely	Substantial
P005153	Matruh Resource Management	1993	Rural	22.0	S	S	Closed	12/31/2002	S	Likely	Substantial
P005168	Private Sector Tourism Infrastructure & Environmental Mgmt Project	1993	Urban Development	130.0	U	S	Closed	12/31/2003	MU	Likely	Modest
P005157	Agricultural Modernization Project	1994	Rural	121.0	U	U	Closed	12/31/2001	MS	Unlikely	Modest
P005173	Irrigation Improvement Project[b]	1995	Rural	80.0	S	MS	Closed	12/31/2006	MS	Significant	NA
P040507	Pollution Abatement Project	1996	Energy and Mining	35.0	S	U	Closed	03/31/2003			
P005163	Population Project	1996	Health, Nutrition and Population	17.2	MS	MS	Closed	03/31/2005	S	Likely	Substantial
P043102	Social Fund Project II	1996	Social Protection	120.0	S	U	Closed	06/30/2001	MS	Unlikely	Modest
P005169	Education Enhancement Program Project[b]	1997	Education	75.0	S	S	Closed	08/31/2006	MS	Significant	NA
P054958	Pollution Abatement Project	1998	Environment	35.0	S	S	Closed	03/30/2005	S	Likely	Substantial
P057704	Port Sector Reform Project	1998	Transport	2.0	U	U	Closed	06/30/2000	NR	NR	NR
P053832	Private Sector and Agriculture Development	1999	Rural	300.0	HU	HU	Closed	08/04/2004	HU	HU	Negligible
P052705	Social Fund for Development Project III[b]	1999	Social Protection	50.0	S	S	Closed	02/28/2006	MS	Moderate	NA
P066336	Social Protection Initiatives Project	1999	Social Protection	5.0	MS	S	Closed	03/30/2005	MS	Likely	Modest
P074075	Second Matruh Resource Management Project	2003	Rural	12.4	S	U	Closed	02/16/2005	NR	NA	NR

Source: World Bank internal database as of October 15, 2007.
Note: **Ratings:** HU = highly unlikely; M = modest; MS = moderately satisfactory; MU = moderately unsatisfactory; NR = not rated; S = satisfactory; U = unsatisfactory. DO = development objective; ID = institutional development; IP = implementation progress.
a. Adjustment lending.
b. These projects closed in fiscal 2006, when IEG's rating system was revised. The "IEG Sustainability" rating changed to "Risk to Development." The "IEG Institutional Development" rating has been incorporated into the outcome rating.
c. Dates indicate either original or revised closing dates.

Table A.4c: World Bank Commitments and Disbursements by Pillar

	Project status	Approval fiscal year	Date, revised closing[a]	IBRD/IDA amount ($ million)	Disbursed ($ million)	Project ID
I–Promotion of High Economic Growth through Structural Reform						
Financial sector						
Financial Sector Development Policy Loan	Active	2006	06/30/2007	500.0	500.0	P088877
Mortgage Finance Project	Active	2007	07/31/2011	37.1	0.0	P093470
Total				**537.1**	**500.0**	
II–Development of Agriculture and Water Resources, Infrastructure, and Environment						
Energy and mining						
Gas Investment Project	Closed	1991	06/30/1999	84.0	84.0	P005111
El Tebbin Power Project	Active	2006	04/30/2011	259.6	36.9	P091945
Environment						
Pollution Abatement Project	Closed	1998	03/30/2005	35.0	35.0	P054958
Pollution Abatement Project II	Active	2006	02/28/2012	20.0	2.0	P090073
Rural sector						
Pumping Stations Rehabilitation Project II	Closed	1990	09/15/1998	31.0	30.3	P005149
National Drainage Project	Closed	1992	12/31/2000	120.0	120.0	P005146
Matruh Resource Management Project	Closed	1993	12/31/2002	22.0	21.6	P005153
Agricultural Modernization Project	Closed	1994	12/31/2001	121.0	100.4	P005157
Irrigation Improvement Project	Closed	1995	12/31/2006	80.0	69.8	P005173
East Delta Newlands Agricultural Services Project	Active	1998	12/31/2008	15.0	9.7	P049166
Sohag Rural Development Project	Active	1999	04/30/2008	25.0	25.0	P040858
Pumping Stations Rehabilitation Project III	Active	1999	08/31/2007	120.0	98.8	P041410
Private Sector and Agriculture Development Project	Closed	1999	08/04/2004	300.0	0.9	P053832
National Drainage Project II	Active	2000	12/31/2008	50.0	45.7	P045499
Matruh Resource Management Project II	Closed	2003	02/16/2005	12.4	0.0	P074075
Integrated Irrigation Improvement and Management Project	Active	2005	03/31/2014	120.0	3.6	P073977
West Delta Water Conservation and Irrigation Rehabilitation Project	Active	2007	06/30/2011	145.0		P087970
Transport						
Port Sector Reform Project	Closed	1998	06/30/2000	2.0	0.0	P057704
Airports Development Project	Active	2004	06/30/2009	335.0	208.4	P082914
Urban development						
Private Sector Tourism Infrastructure & Environmental Management Project	Closed	1993	12/31/2003	130.0	62.4	P005168
Total				**2,027.0**	**954.5**	

(*Continued on the following page*)

Table A.4c: World Bank Commitments and Disbursements by Pillar (*continued*)

	Project status	Approval fiscal year	Date, revised closing[a]	IBRD/IDA amount ($ million)	Disbursed ($ million)	Project ID
III–Development of Human Resources						
Education						
Engineering and Technical Education Project	Closed	1990	12/31/1998	30.5	29.4	P005140
Basic Education Improvement Project	Closed	1993	12/31/2003	55.5	49.3	P005161
Education Enhancement Project	Closed	1997	08/31/2006	75.0	76.3	P005169
Secondary Education Enhancement Project	Active	1999	06/30/2010	50.0	26.7	P050484
Higher Education Enhancement Project	Active	2002	12/31/2008	50.0	39.0	P056236
Skills Development Project	Active	2004	06/30/2010	5.5	1.4	P049702
Early Childhood Education Enhancement Project	Active	2005	12/31/2010	20.0	1.1	P082952
Health, nutrition, and population						
National Schistosomiasis Control Project	Closed	1992	09/30/2002	26.8	21.4	P005152
Population Project	Closed	1996	03/31/2005	17.2	15.1	P005163
Health Sector Reform	Active	1998	03/31/2009	90.0	92.6	P045175
Social protection						
Social Fund Project II	Closed	1996	06/30/2001	120.0	120.0	P043102
Social Fund Project III	Closed	1999	02/28/2006	50.0	50.0	P052705
Social Protection Initiatives Project	Closed	1999	03/30/2005	5.0	4.9	P066336
Total				**595.5**	**527.2**	
Grand total				**3,159.6**	**1,981.7**	

Source: CASs and World Bank internal database as of September 25, 2007.

a. Dates indicate either original or revised closing dates.

Table A.5: Delivered Analytical and Advisory Work, Fiscal 1997–2007

Name	Delivered fiscal year
I–Promotion of high economic growth through structural reform	
Macro	
Country Economic Memorandum: Issues in Sustaining Economic Growth	1997
Social and Structural Review	2001
Trade and tariffs	
Export Development Strategy Note	1997
Trade Policy Developments in MENA	2000
Toward Agricultural Competitiveness in the 21st Century—An Agricultural Export-Oriented Strategy	2001
Export Promotion Task Force Report	2001
Private and financial sector	
FSAP: Reviews, Lessons, and Issues Going Forward	2003
Policy Note on Pension Reform	2005
Public Land Management Strategy	2006
Access to Finance	2006
ICA: Towards a Better Investment Climate for Growth and Employment Creation	2006
ICA Follow up	2007
FSAP Update	2007
Public sector and governance	
Partners for Development: New Roles for Government and Private Sector in MENA	2000
ROSC Accounting and Auditing	2003
Country Procurement Assessment Report update	2004
Country Financial Accountability Assessment	2004
Institutional Financial Management Capacity Assessment	2005
Public Expenditure Review Notes	
Fiscal and Public Debt Sustainability	2005
Budget Construction	2006
Intergovernmental Relations and Fiscal Decentralization	2006
Working papers	
Deep integration, Nondiscrimination, and Euro-Mediterranean Free Trade	1999
Economic Reforms in Egypt: Emerging Patterns and Their Possible Implications	1999
Commercial Banking and Microfinance in Egypt: National Bank for Development—Case Study	2000
Politically Optimal Tariffs: An Application to Egypt	2003
ROSC Corporate Governance Country Assessment	2004
Fiscal and Public Debt Sustainability in Egypt	2005
Economic Growth in Egypt: Constraints and Determinants	2006
The Welfare Effects of a Large Depreciation: The Case of Egypt, 2000–05	2007
II–Development of agriculture and water resources, infrastructure, and environment	
Water	
Water Sector Notes	2000
Integrated Water Resources Management Plan	2005

(*Continued on the following page*)

Table A.5: Delivered Analytical and Advisory Work, Fiscal 1997–2007 (*continued*)

Name	Delivered fiscal year
Operational Framework for Integrated Rural Sanitation Service Delivery	2005
Public Expenditure Review Note: Cost Effectiveness and Equity in Egypt's Water Sector	2005
Environment	
Gulf of Aqaba Environment Action Plan	2000
Cost Assessment of Environmental Degradation	2002
Country Environmental Analysis (1992–2002)	2005
Nile Basin Regional Initiative	Dropped
Infrastructure	
Cairo Urban Transport Note	1999
Public Expenditure Review Note: Restructuring Egypt's Railways	2006
Urban Sector Strategy	2007
Economic Costs of Gas in Egypt	2007
Road Asset Management	2007
Working papers	
Case of Urbanization and Industrialization in Shubra el-Kheima, Egypt	2000
Nile River Basin: Transboundary Environmental Analysis	2001
Balancing Productivity and Environmental Pressure in Egypt: Toward an Interdisciplinary and Integrated Approach to Agricultural Drainage	2004
Connecting Residential Households to Natural Gas: An Economic and Financial Analysis	2006
Assessing the Economic Impacts of Climate Change on Agriculture in Egypt: A Ricardian Approach	2008
III–Development of human resources	
Health	
Health Sector Reform	1998
Toward a Virtuous Circle: A Nutrition Review of MENA	2000
Egypt Governorate Health Plan	2002
Egypt Health Sector Review and Financing Study	2004
Public Expenditure Review Note: Health Policy Note	2006
Education	
Comprehensive Development Framework for Education and Training	2001
Strategic Options for Early Childhood Education	2002
Education Sector Review: Progress and Priorities for the Future (Vols. I and II)	2002
Education Sector Strategy Note	2007
Public Expenditure Review Notes:	
Making Egyptian Education Spending More Effective	2005
Capital Investment in the Education Sector	2006
Managing Textbook Expenditure	2006
Poverty and social protection	
Safety Net Task Force Report	2001
Poverty Reduction in Egypt-Diagnosis and Strategy (Vols. I and II)	2002
Egypt Country Gender Assessment	2003

Table A.5: Delivered Analytical and Advisory Work, Fiscal 1997–2007

Name		Delivered fiscal year
A Poverty Reduction Strategy for Egypt		2004
Redesigning the Subsidies: Poverty & Social Impact Analysis		2006
Upper-Egypt Challenges and Priorities for Rural Development		2006
Poverty Assessment Update		2007
Working papers		
Education in MENA: A Strategy Towards Learning for Development		1999
Making Microfinance Work in MENA		1999
Egypt: Reforming Vocational Education and Training to Meet Private Sector Skill Demands		1999
Self-Targeted Subsidies-The Distributional Impact of the Egyptian Food Subsidy System		2000
Poverty and Economic Growth in Egypt, 1995–2000		2003
The Economics of Tobacco in Egypt: A New Analysis of Demand		2003
Increasing Girls' School Enrollment in the Arab Republic of Egypt		2004
Egypt and the Millennium Development Goals: Challenges and Opportunities		2005
Reimbursable technical assistance	**Fiscal year**	**Project status**
Pension Reform Program	2006	A
Ministry of Communication and Information Support	2008	A
National Post Organization Support	2008	A
Information Technology Industry Development Agency Support	2008	A
National Telecom Regulatory Authority	2007	C
Regulatory Reform, Governance and Investment Support	2007	A

Source: World Bank.
Note: ICA = investment climate assessment; FSAP = Financial Sector Assessment Program; MENA = Middle East and North Africa; ROSC = Report on the Observance and Standards of Codes.

Table A.6a: Project Ratings for Egypt and Comparator Countries, Fiscal 1999–2007

	Total evaluated		Outcome—% satisfactory		Institutional development impact—% substantial		Sustainability—% likely	
Country	$ million	Number	$	Number	$	Number	$	Number
Egypt, Arab Rep. of	904.3	20	89.7	83.3	51	46.7	63.5	73.3
Algeria	550.8	19	62.5	68.4	41	30.8	49.7	50.0
Indonesia	8,016.3	89	66.8	65.5	31	35.4	51.4	44.3
Morocco	1,698.6	30	63.2	73.3	34	30.0	74.7	88.9
Tunisia	1,579.1	26	95.9	92.3	55	68.0	96.8	95.8
Turkey	5,966.7	34	92.9	90.9	66	48.4	90.8	78.6
Middle East and North Africa	7,320.0	189	81.1	75.3	45	37.6	80.7	72.1
World Bank	163,533.0	2,367	80.4	76.1	54	49.6	80.6	73.2

Source: World Bank internal database as of December 19, 2007.

Table A.6b: Portfolio Status Indicators: Egypt and Comparators, as of End 2007

	Number of projects	Net commitment amount ($ million)	Number of projects at risk	Commitment at risk ($ million)	% commitment at risk
Egypt, Arab Rep. of	15	1,321.6	2	140.0	10.6
Algeria	3	45.1	2	26.7	59.2
Indonesia	25	2,741.8	4	304.5	11.1
Morocco	12	747.4	2	53.2	7.1
Tunisia	13	670.1	0	0.0	0.0
Turkey	22	5,639.5	2	429.0	7.6
Middle East and North Africa	93	5,860.8	16	1,087.7	18.6
World Bank	1,347	97,790.5	224	15,175.6	15.5

Source: World Bank internal database as of December 19, 2007.

Table A.7: World Bank's Senior Management, 1999–2007

Year	Vice president	Resident representative	Country coordinator
1999	Kemal Dervis	Khalid Ikram	Richard Westin
2000	Jean-Louis Sarbib	Mahmood A. Ayub	Mae Chu Chang (acting)
2001	Jean-Louis Sarbib	Mahmood A. Ayub	John Mcgregor
2002	Jean-Louis Sarbib	Mahmood A. Ayub	John Mcgregor
2003	Jean-Louis Sarbib	Mahmood A. Ayub	Habib Fetini
2004	Christiaan Poortman	Mahmood A. Ayub	Habib Fetini
2005	Christiaan Poortman	Emmanuel Mbi	Gaiv Tata
2006	Daniela Gressani	Emmanuel Mbi	Gaiv Tata
2007	Daniela Gressani	Emmanuel Mbi	Xavier Devictor

Source: World Bank directories.

Table A.8: Bank Budget by Cost Category and Comparator Countries, Fiscal 1999–2007 ($ million)

	Fiscal year											
	1999	2000	2001	2002	2003	2004	2005	2006	2007	Average	Total	Budget distrib. %
Egypt, Arab Rep. of												
Project supervision	1.3	1.5	1.3	1.5	1.2	1.3	1.4	1.5	2.1	1.5	13.1	33.3
Lending	1.8	0.6	0.4	0.7	0.8	1.1	1.9	2.4	1.9	1.3	11.6	29.5
ESW	0.4	0.7	0.8	1.2	1.2	1.1	2.0	1.7	2.4	1.3	11.5	29.2
Other	0.0	0.7	0.1	0.1	0.3	0.3	0.5	0.6	0.5	0.3	3.1	8.0
Country services	3.5	3.6	2.6	3.5	3.5	3.8	5.8	6.2	6.9	4.4	39.4	100.0
Turkey												
Project supervision	1.9	2.5	2.4	3.4	2.8	1.9	2.4	2.8	3.0	2.6	23.1	36.7
Lending	1.3	2.4	2.0	2.5	1.9	3.1	2.9	2.2	1.7	2.2	20.1	31.9
ESW	0.9	1.1	0.9	1.8	1.4	1.7	1.7	3.6	2.2	1.7	15.3	24.4
Other	0.0	0.4	0.3	0.3	0.4	0.6	0.9	0.8	0.7	0.5	4.4	7.0
Country services	4.1	6.4	5.5	8.0	6.6	7.3	8.0	9.3	7.6	7.0	62.9	100.0
Indonesia												
Project supervision	4.9	6.2	4.3	5.0	4.3	4.4	3.6	4.1	4.3	4.6	41.2	37.9
Lending	3.5	1.9	1.8	1.9	2.7	4.6	3.5	4.4	3.7	3.1	28.0	25.8
ESW	3.0	3.8	3.1	3.8	3.6	2.9	3.4	4.9	3.9	3.6	32.4	29.9
Other	0.1	0.4	1.0	1.0	1.2	1.2	0.7	0.7	0.7	0.8	6.9	6.4
Country services	11.5	12.2	10.2	11.7	11.8	13.2	11.2	14.1	12.6	12.1	108.6	100.0
Middle East and North Africa Region												
Project supervision	10.1	11.2	10.4	10.7	10.5	11.3	12.8	12.2	13.5	11.4	102.8	25.5
Lending	8.8	11.2	8.4	9.3	6.4	9.0	9.9	11.1	8.8	9.2	82.8	20.6
ESW	6.4	10.4	10.2	14.5	20.6	22.6	20.4	22.4	22.1	16.6	149.5	37.2
Other	2.2	4.0	4.9	6.8	6.8	8.3	8.9	13.1	12.2	7.5	67.3	16.7
Country services	27.5	36.8	34.0	41.3	44.3	51.2	52.0	58.8	56.5	44.7	402.3	100.0
World Bank												
Project supervision	127.6	158.8	136.4	152.4	160.4	167.2	178.2	189.9	199.0	163.3	1,469.8	31.6
Lending	110.4	124.2	102.1	123.2	119.9	156.2	151.3	155.3	148.8	132.4	1,191.2	25.6
ESW	83.1	107.6	88.2	129.8	150.6	154.8	158.3	169.0	162.9	133.8	1,204.3	25.9
Other	42.0	65.6	75.7	86.3	92.1	107.4	102.6	106.3	107.5	87.3	785.4	16.9
Country services	363.1	456.2	402.4	491.6	523.0	585.7	590.3	620.7	618.8	516.9	4,651.8	100.0

Source: World Bank internal database as of November 29, 2007.
Note: ESW = economic and sector work.

Table A.9: Egypt—Millennium Development Goals

	Year			
	1990	**1995**	**2000**	**2005**
Goal 1: Eradicate extreme poverty and hunger				
Income share held by lowest 20%	*8.6*	8.8	8.6	—
Malnutrition prevalence, weight for age (% of children younger than 5)	10.4	16.8	4.0	*8.6*
Poverty gap at $1 a day (PPP) (%)	*0.5*	0.5	0.5	—
Poverty headcount ratio at $1 a day (PPP) (% of population)	*4.0*	2.6	3.1	—
Poverty headcount ratio at national poverty line (% of population)	—	*22.9*	16.7	—
Prevalence of undernourishment (% of population)	*4*	*3*	—	*4*
Goal 2: Achieve universal primary education				
Literacy rate, youth total (% of people ages 15–24)	61	—	—	*85*
Persistence to grade 5, total (% of cohort)	—	—	99	*99*
Primary completion rate, total (% of relevant age group)	—	—	97	*95*
School enrollment, primary (% net)	*84*	—	93	*95*
Goal 3: Promote gender equality and empower women				
Proportion of seats held by women in national Parliament (%)	4	2	2	3
Ratio of girls to boys in primary and secondary education (%)	*79*	—	—	—
Ratio of young literate females to males (% ages 15–24)	*72*	—	—	*88*
Share of women employed in the nonagricultural sector (% of total nonagricultural employment)	20.5	18.9	19.0	*20.6*
Goal 4: Reduce child mortality				
Immunization, measles (% of children ages 12–23 months)	86	89	98	98
Mortality rate, infant (per 1,000 live births)	76	56	40	28
Mortality rate, under-5 (per 1,000)	104	71	49	33
Goal 5: Improve maternal health				
Births attended by skilled health staff (% of total)	*37*	46	61	74
Maternal mortality ratio (modeled estimate, per 100,000 live births)	—	—	84	—
Goal 6: Combat HIV/AIDS, malaria, and other diseases				
Contraceptive prevalence (% of women ages 15–49)	*48*	*55*	*52*	59
Incidence of tuberculosis (per 100,000 people)	36	36	31	25
Prevalence of HIV, female (% ages 15–24)	—	—	—	—
Prevalence of HIV, total (% of population ages 15–49)	—	—	—	0.1
Tuberculosis cases detected under DOTS (%)	—	44	45	63
Goal 7: Ensure environmental sustainability				
CO2 emissions (metric tons per capita)	1.4	1.6	2.1	*2.0*
Forest area (% of land area)	0	—	0	0
GDP per unit of energy use (constant 2000 PPP $ per kilogram of oil equivalent)	5.1	5.2	5.3	*4.9*
Improved sanitation facilities (% of population with access)	54	—	—	*70*
Improved water source (% of population with access)	94	—	—	*98*
Nationally protected areas (% of total land area)	—	—	—	*5.6*

Table A.9: Egypt—Millennium Development Goals

	Year			
	1990	**1995**	**2000**	**2005**
Goal 8: Develop a global partnership for development				
Aid per capita (current $)	97	33	20	13
Debt service (PPG and IMF only, % of exports of G&S, excl. workers' remittances)	23.7	14.6	8.5	6.2
Fixed line and mobile phone subscribers (per 1,000 people)	29	44	102	325
Internet users (per 1,000 people)	0	0	7	68
Personal computers (per 1,000 people)	—	4	12	38
Total debt service (% of exports of goods, services and income)	20.4	13.2	8.5	6.8
Unemployment, youth female (% of female labor force ages 15–24)	—	—	*51.1*	—
Unemployment, youth male (% of male labor force ages 15–24)	—	—	*19.2*	—
Unemployment, youth total (% of total labor force ages 15–24)	—	—	*27.7*	—
Other				
Fertility rate, total (births per woman)	4.3	3.6	3.4	3.1
GNI per capita, Atlas method (current $)	760	930	1,450	1,260
GNI, Atlas method (current $) (billions)	42.5	57.0	97.4	93.0
Gross capital formation (% of GDP)	28.8	20.1	19.6	18.0
Life expectancy at birth, total (years)	63	66	69	71
Literacy rate, adult total (% of people ages 15 and older)	47	—	—	*71*
Population, total (millions)	55.7	61.2	67.3	74.0
Trade (% of GDP)	52.8	50.2	39.0	63.2

Source: World Development Indicators database.

Note: Figures in italics are for years other than those specified. — = data are not available. DOTS = Development Outcome Tracking System; GDP = gross domestic product; IMF = International Monetary Fund; PPG = public and publicly guaranteed; PPP = public-private partnership.

The Bank's efforts aim to reduce gender disparities; significant progress was made through a number of projects in education reform for girls. Photo courtesy World Bank Group.

Summary

Since 2004 Egypt has made significant strides in improving its business climate and in attracting foreign investment. However, there remains an unfinished reform agenda, especially in the financial sector. During the Country Assistance Strategy (CAS) review period (1997–2007), the International Finance Corporation's (IFC) strategy has been to support the private sector and build an efficient financial sector. IFC operations—investment as well as advisory—were broadly consistent with that strategy. Collaboration between IFC and the International Bank for Reconstruction and Development (IBRD) in Egypt has been good. Challenges ahead include the continued need for regulatory reforms, quality enhancement in advisory services, power sector reforms, increased levels of investment, inadequacies in infrastructure, and financial sector reforms.

Private Sector and Business Climate

The Egyptian economy has recovered from the recession of 2001–03. Egypt is a lower-middle-income[3] country, with a per capita income of $1,350 (2006) and is home to the largest population in the Arab world (71 million in January 2007). Since 1997, Egypt has been in an uneven but gradual transition to a more open, market-oriented economy. Following September 11, 2001, a slump in tourism and a decline in foreign exchange reserves led to a 45 percent fall in the currency between 2000 and 2003, rising interest rates, and an economic slowdown. After weathering a recession between 2001 and 2003, the economy recovered strongly.[4] Structural reforms[5] implemented since 2004 have led to a strong revival of the economy (gross domestic product [GDP] growth in 2006 was 6.8 percent), marked by a stable external position, surging capital flows, a market-determined currency, rallying asset values, falling inflation rates, sliding unemployment, and more optimistic expectations and investor sentiment.

The investment climate in Egypt has steadily improved. Egypt has remained a medium-risk country during the review period. Overall, the investment climate in the country has improved, based on both the Institutional Investor Country Credit Risk Ratings and the Heritage Foundation Index (figure B.1).[6] According to the 2007 investment climate assessment update, businesses identified macroeconomic instability, anticompetitive practices, and corruption as the top three constraints[7] (table B.1). The improvement in investment climate also comes through, when the investment climate assessments from 2007 and 2005 are compared, especially with regard to tax issues.

Egypt topped the list of reformers in the latest (2008)* Doing Business *report. During 2006, Egypt undertook reforms in the protection of property rights and business regulations to make them more business friendly and its overall *Doing Business* rankings improved (table B.2). Egypt cut the minimum capital required to start a business, from 50,000 Egyptian pounds to just 1,000, and halved the time and cost of start-up. It reduced fees for registering property from 3 percent of the property value to a low, fixed amount. It eased the bureaucracy in getting construction permits. It launched new one-stop shops at Egyptian ports, cutting the time to import by seven days and the time to export by five days and it established a new private credit bureau.[8] As a result of these reforms, Egypt

Figure B.1: Investment Climate in Egypt, 1999–2007

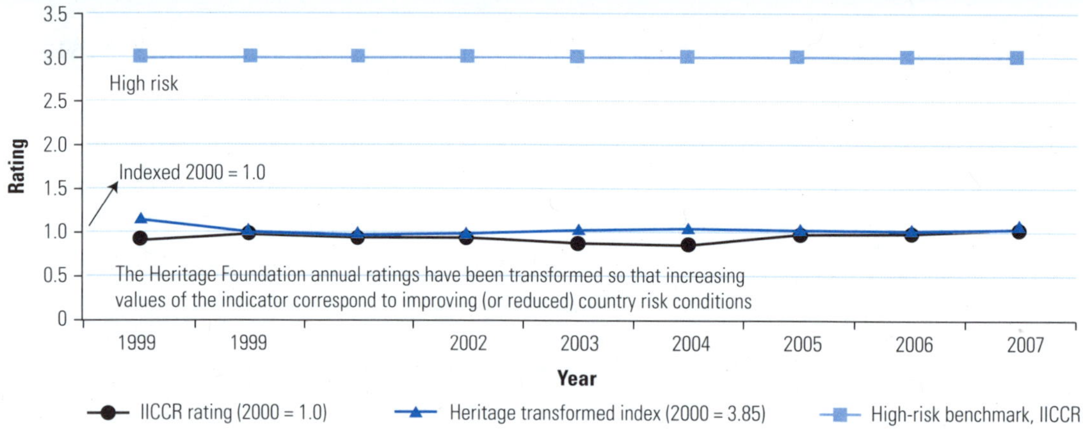

Source: IFC.

moved up 26 places, from a rank of 152 (of 178) in 2006 to 126 in 2007.

Investment climate improvements have boosted private capital flows and the stock market. Egyptian reforms in streamlining investment procedures have played a key role in improving the outlook for investment. Private capital flows and foreign direct investment (FDI) increased nearly five-fold since 2001 (table B.3). According to the 2007 *World Investment Report* (UNCTAD 2007), Egypt has emerged as the lead FDI recipient country in the African continent.[9] The Egyptian stock market also boomed in 2005 and 2006[10] (table B.3) in the wake of the implementation of a strong economic reform agenda that led to a drastic improvement of public expectations about the country's economic future—including strong future corporate earnings and a higher growth trajectory (Billmeier and Massa 2007). It has been also bolstered by the investment of Gulf oil capital.

Table B.1: Top 10 Constraints to Firm Investment in Egypt, 2006

	% of firms identifying problem as "major" or "very severe" obstacle		
	Egypt 2006	**Egypt 2004**	**Middle East & North Africa 2005**
Macroeconomic instability	70	73	57
Anticompetitive or informal practices "illegal competition"	65	56	
Corruption[a]	62	50	
Regulatory policy uncertainty	60	64	55
Tax rates	53	79	50
Cost of financing	41	42	31
Tax administration	39	59	41
Skills/education of available workers	36	28	
Labor regulations	31	27	12
Access to financing	26	33	24

Sources: World Bank 2005e; Allaoua 2005.

a. According to the 2006 investment climate assessment, this constraint was framed differently in the 2006 survey for unknown reasons; hence, the comparison is somewhat less reliable.

Table B.2: Doing Business Ratings for Egypt, 2007 and 2008

Ease of...	2008 rank	2007 rank	Change in rank
Doing business	126	152	+26
Starting a business	55	126	+71
Dealing with licenses	163	165	+2
Employing workers	108	106	–2
Registering property	101	147	+46
Getting credit	115	156	+41
Protecting investors	83	105	+22
Paying taxes	150	152	+2
Trading across borders	26	86	+60
Enforcing contracts	145	146	+1
Closing a business	125	124	–1

Source: www.doingbusiness.org.
Note: Doing Business 2007 rankings have been recalculated to reflect changes to the methodology and the addition of three new countries.

Privatization of state-owned enterprises has remained a priority. Privatization of state-owned enterprises has been a key component of the government's reform program. According to the World Bank's privatization database, between 2000 and 2005, the government privatized 22 enterprises in a range of sectors, including manufacturing, infrastructure, energy, telecommunications, and finance. However, the share of the private sector in GDP has not increased significantly over the last decade. As of October 2007, 82 companies were listed for sale by the government (www.investment.gov.eg), comprising 39 companies (or stakes in companies) and 43 joint ventures.

However, there remains an unfinished reform agenda, especially in the financial sector.

Banking sector: Banks account for more than 60 percent of the assets of the financial system (World Bank 2006a). Credit to the private sector averaged 59 percent of GDP during the 1999–2006 period (table B.3), well above the Middle East and North Africa average of 40 percent and slightly above the middle-income country average of 57 percent. According to the investment climate assessment, access to finance was a serious problem in Egypt in 2006, with only 11 percent of private sector firms in Egypt having an outstanding loan from a bank/financial institution (figure B.2). The data suggest that credit to the private sector is highly concentrated.

The finance problem is especially severe for small and medium enterprises (SMEs),[11] with only 7 percent of small firms borrowing from banks/financial institutions[12] (15 percent for medium and 23 percent for large firms). Also, only 4 percent (6.2 percent in 2004) of the surveyed firms got working capital finance from commercial banks. The banking industry is dominated by state-owned banks that account for more than 58 percent of total deposits.[13] Furthermore, the portfolios of the government-owned banks—mostly made up of government securities with short maturities[14] and the guaranteed income from the large-scale government borrowings—substantially reduce the banks' incentives to develop capacity and assessment techniques to serve the private sector and especially SMEs.

Nonbank financial sector. Egypt's nonbank financial institutions are underdeveloped. They are composed of a stock exchange—sizeable in terms of market capitalization (47 percent of GDP; table B.3) but having small trading volumes—with a low turnover ratio (28 percent;

Figure B.2: Egyptian Firms' Access to Credit

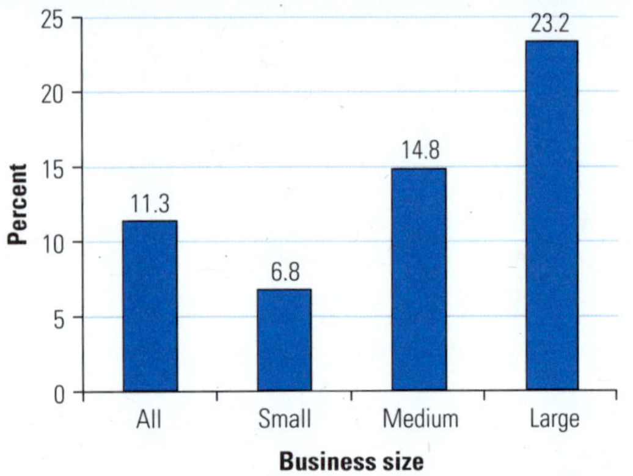

Source: World Bank (2007a).

table B.3) and a relatively small contractual savings sector including insurance, funded pensions, and mutual funds and underdeveloped mortgage and ancillary financial institutions. Combined insurance and private pension funds under management amounted only to 8 percent of GDP in June 2004.

The housing finance market continues to face challenges because of issues related to high fees and inefficient procedures for land registration, weak regulatory authority, and poor access to long-term credit. The financial leasing industry is represented by only seven companies operating with low annual volumes of leases, the result of an inadequate property registration system, high stamp duties, and an ineffective tax judicial system.[15] Venture capital and factoring are virtually nonexistent, although some related financial services are being provided by banks.

IFC Objectives/Strategy in Egypt

IFC's strategy in Egypt has been to support the private sector and build an efficient financial sector.

CAS I (1997–2000)

The 1997 CAS was one of the earliest joint CASs between IBRD and IFC. The strategic objectives of the CAS included export development, private sector-led growth, development of human resources, and natural resource management. IFC was expected to continue to play an important role in supporting individual investments in private and privatizing companies, manufacturing, infrastructure, power, oil and gas, tourism, agribusiness, and the financial sector. IFC investments were expected to catalyze other investments and have a demonstration effect on foreign and domestic investors.

CAS II (2001–05)

The theme of this CAS was to reduce poverty and unemployment. The 2001 joint CAS noted that IFC's priorities, closely coordinated with the Bank's activities, would emphasize more rapid job creation through private sector use of natural resources for sustainable development. It described IFC as seeking additional investments in support of (i) developing private sector-financed infrastructure; (ii) providing support to the services sector, including tourism; (iii) financing internationally competitive and export-oriented ventures; and (iv) supporting the government's privatization effort through both advisory services to particular transactions and financing for privatized ventures. Other possible areas of IFC involvement included supporting SMEs, developing financial markets, and participating in building pipelines to export Egypt's large natural gas reserves to Eastern Mediterranean countries.

CAS III (2006–09)

The strategic objectives reflected in this CAS included facilitating private sector development, enhancing the provision of public services, and promoting equity. The 2005 CAS stated that IFC will focus on (i) supporting private participation in infrastructure initiatives with guarantees, capital, or advisory services as required; (ii) assisting in the development of new financial sector institutions and instruments for the private sector; (iii) catalyzing new private sector investment in manufacturing, petro-chemicals, oil and gas, as well as the social sectors; and (iv) supporting SME initiatives. IFC was also expected to facilitate cross-

Figure B.3: IFC Commitments in Egypt, Fiscal 1997–2007 ($ millions)

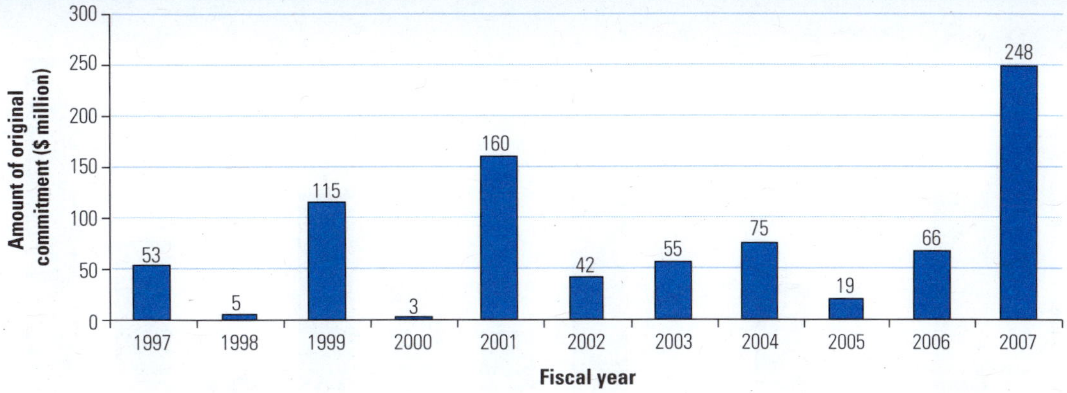

Source: IFC, MIS data system.
Note: Figures reflect the original commitments.

border investments into Egypt and to support the expansion of the internationally competitive Egyptian companies into new markets (South-South investments). It was expected that there would continue to be a demand for IFC financing in power generation. IFC was expected to explore the scope for private participation in power distribution and to develop alternative sources for generation such as wind power.

In advisory services, the Private Enterprise Partnership for the Middle East and North Africa Region (PEP-MENA) was expected to be the main vehicle to provide technical assistance for the financial sector, support to SMEs, assistance for improvement of the business-enabling environment, support to development of public-private partnerships (PPPs) (particularly for infrastructure), and assistance in privatizing or restructuring state-owned enterprises.

IFC Activities and Results, 1997–2007

Between 1997 and 2007, IFC committed 57 investment operations totaling $842 million and 37 advisory operations for $12 million.

Investment operations

Between 1997 and 2007, IFC invested in 57 projects for $842 million in new commitments (figures B.3 and B.4 and table B.4), with 14 percent of the amount in equity and 86 percent in loans. Except for fiscal 2001 and 2007—when IFC committed $153 million and $248 million, respectively—IFC's commitments between fiscal 1997 and 2007 averaged about $76 million annually.[16] As of December 2007 the portfolio is diversified and includes investments in the financial sector, power,[17] manufacturing, ports, oil and gas, metals, agribusiness, mining, information technology, and health care. Financial markets account for 30 percent of the number of investments and 21 percent of dollar volume, and infrastructure accounts for 13 percent of the dollar volume.

IEG reviewed 13 of the 19 investments committed between 1997 and 2002 that attained operational maturity between 2002 and 2007.[18] Of these, seven had successful development outcome and investment outcome ratings. Successful projects demonstrated market leadership and the ability to respond to changing conditions. However, sponsors of unsuccessful projects lacked experience, could not manage new technology, and underestimated implementation risk.

Figure B.4: IFC Commitments in Egypt: Fiscal 1997–2007 (number of investments)

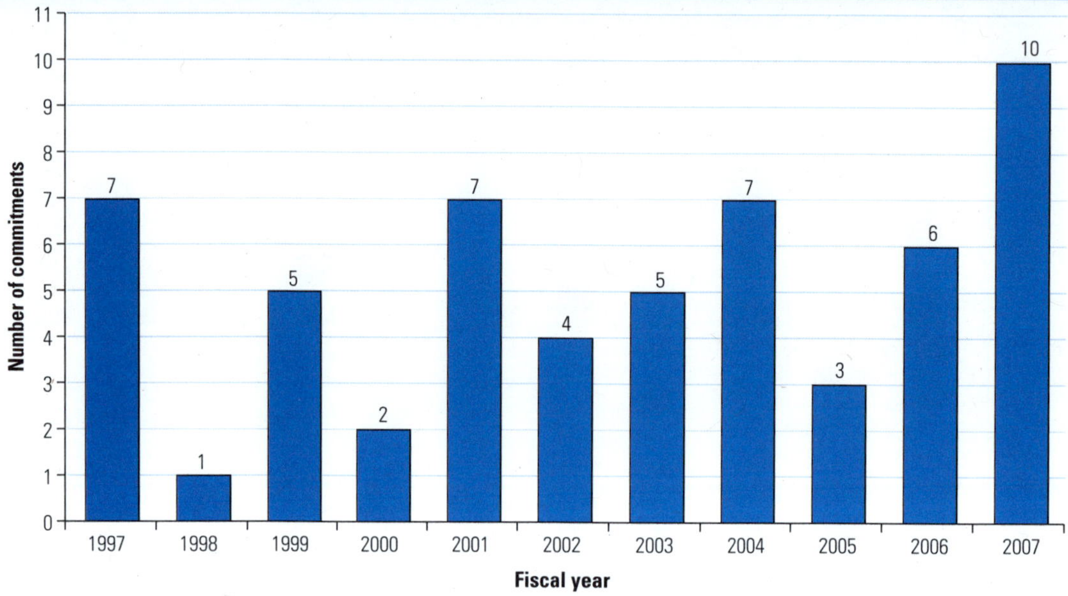

Source: IFC, MIS data system.
Note: IFC = International Finance Corporation.

Figure B.5 compares IFC commitments in Egypt, FDI flows to Egypt, and Egypt's GDP, in relation to developing countries for the 1997–2006 period. Between 1997 and 2005, Egypt accounted for 0.7 percent of the FDI flows to developing countries, but 2.1 percent of IFC commitments to developing countries. Likewise, Egypt's 1.9 percent share of IFC commitments to developing countries for the 1997–2006 period exceeded its 1.2 percent share of developing countries' GDP. In other words, Egypt's share of IFC commitments to developing countries for the 1997–2006 period exceeded the benchmarks for its share of FDI and GDP.

Advisory services

Between 1997 and 2007, IFC undertook 37 advisory services operations[19] in Egypt for about $12 million (table B.5), with a rapid build-up of the portfolio in recent years. The advisory services operations are evenly spread (in number) across the five business lines—Access to Finance, Business Enabling Environment, Environment and Social Sustainability, Infrastructure, and Value Addition to Firms. However, in terms of dollar volume, Infrastructure tops the list, with 46 percent of the total, and Environment and Social Sustainability is the smallest at 9 percent.[20]

In addition, the Foreign Investment Advisory Service carried out the following four assignments during the review period: develop an FDI database for $153,000 (1999); develop a strategy for investment promotion for $175,000 (2000); assist the government in facilitating private investment and improving transparency and effectiveness of government operations—$100,000 in 2001; and (iv) review the Free Zone Policy of Egypt for $202,000 (2005).

Assessment

Except for spikes in investments in 1999, 2001, and 2007, the level of IFC investments in Egypt has been modest during the review period in supporting private sector development. The level increased sharply in fiscal 2007, following the reforms of 2004. Although IFC supported

Figure B.5: IFC Commitments, FDI, and GDP—Egypt and Developing Countries, 1997–2006

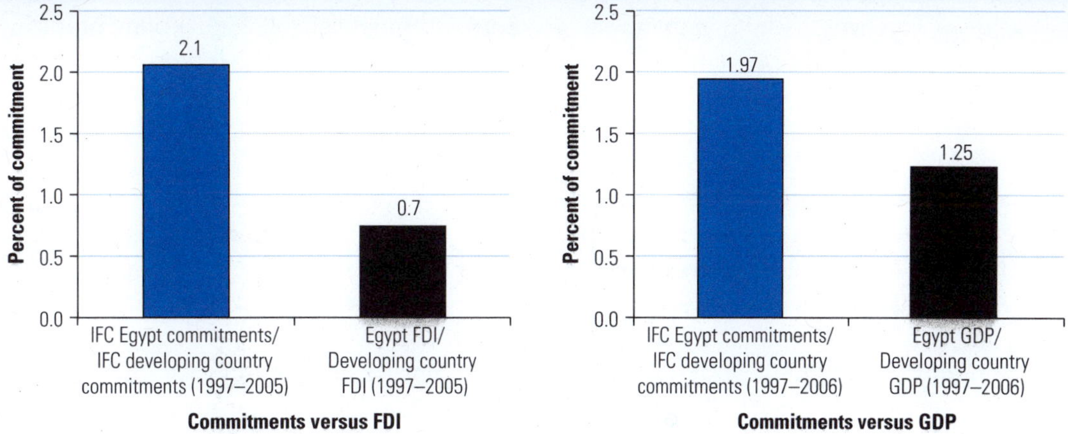

Source: IFC, MIS data system.
Note: FDI = foreign direct investment; GDP = gross domestic product; IFC = International Finance Corporation.

manufacturing enterprises[21] throughout the review period, because of the dominant role of the public sector until the reforms of 2004, IFC activity in the financial sector was limited;[22] it has picked up since. IFC-supported investments have been largely successful and the credit risk ratings of recent loan and equity commitments are positive.[23] Egypt's share of IFC commitments to developing countries for the 1997–2006 period exceeded the benchmarks for its share of FDI and GDP.

IFC's Contributions to CAS Goals

IFC activities during the review period were consistent with IFC priorities and CAS objectives.

CAS I (1997–2000)

Although IFC activities during this CAS period were consistent with IFC priorities and CAS strategic objectives, they were more modest than IFC had anticipated (see table B.6). IFC committed 15 investments for $177 million (table B.4).

In the financial sector, IFC focused on the creation of new specialized financial institutions and approved investments in the first private joint venture life insurance company and an investment bank. IFC also helped to establish an offshore closed-end fund investing in listed Egyptian equities.

In the industrial sector, IFC invested in companies producing steel, cement, carbon black, industrial gases, and corrugated boxes. In tourism, IFC invested in two integrated tourist resorts on the Red Sea coast.

IFC advisory services during the CAS period included conducting the financial and technical assessment of an integrated steel mill and arranging the financing for the company's investments to produce flat products and providing advice on removing impediments to local bond market development, with financing from the Technical Assistance Trust Funds.

As the IFC operations were modest, they had limited impact on promoting private sector-led growth.

CAS II (2001–05)

During the CAS II period, IFC committed 26 investments for $351 million (table B.4). IFC supported SMEs through the North Africa Enterprise Development—set up in April 2003 and transformed as PEP-MENA in October 2004—and provided technical assistance to the leading microfinance nongovernmental organization in Egypt to help implement a credit-scoring tool and improve its risk management framework. IFC also launched a microfinance pilot project in Upper Egypt with a leading commercial bank. IFC invested in the country's first private sector housing bank and in one of the first leasing companies. IFC established the Egyptian trade facility and set up the first factoring company in Egypt.

In infrastructure, IFC invested in two independent power producers (IPPs) to build and operate power plants. IFC's support to the services sector included an investment in the supermarket sector. IFC invested in a number of export-oriented[24] companies, including an organic producer of pharmaceuticals, an auto parts manufacturer, and a ceramic tiles company. IFC supported a number of privatized companies—in both financial and nonfinancial sectors—during the CAS period.

IFC activities during the CAS II period were consistent with the IFC priorities (table B.6) and though still modest, they increased in commitment volume over the previous CAS period.

CAS III (2006–09)

IFC investments during this CAS period have supported the priorities identified and the strategic objectives (see table B.6). During the first two years of this CAS period, IFC committed 16 investments for $314.7 million (table B.4). The main focus for IFC in the financial sector has been to make it more competitive and efficient. Key interventions include equity investments in privatized banks and a mortgage finance company; advisory work to improve corporate governance through training of bank directors; and supporting improvements in Egypt's financial infrastructure through the establishment of the first private credit bureau.

In the area of increasing trade, IFC has signed with several local banks' trade finance facilities under the Global Trade Finance Program and has financed the expansion of the Sokhna Port, an IFC investee. IFC is active in improving the business-enabling environment through its PEP-MENA work, including the technical assistance launched with the General Authority for Investment and Free Zones to reform business registration and licensing procedures in early 2006 for supporting business start-up simplification in Alexandria. IFC also supported a number of investments that were planning to expand their businesses on a Regional basis.

In the area of infrastructure services, IFC has signed a mandate with the Ministry of Finance for a freeway project. In the health sector, IFC has signed a mandate with the Ministry of Finance for a hospital PPP project and to support PPPs for the construction and management of two new public hospitals. In fiscal 2007, IFC invested in two hospitals and a health care group. In the education sector, IFC is advising the Ministries of Finance and Education to support PPPs for the construction and management of new public schools. In the water sector, IFC is expected to provide transaction advice for PPPs regarding the concessioning of a potable water treatment plant for New Cairo. Through its PEP-MENA program, IFC is active in increasing opportunities for women.

IFC activities during the current CAS period seem consistent with the IFC priorities. IFC activities in Egypt have increased significantly, with Egypt becoming IFC's largest Middle East and North Africa client—overtaking long-standing top client, Pakistan—in fiscal 2007.

Overall, collaboration between IFC and IBRD in Egypt has improved. Since 2004, IFC-IBRD collaboration has picked up[25] because of a shift in government policy to an emphasis on private sector development and PPPs. IFC's presence in Cairo, where IFC's hub[26] in the Middle East and North Africa Region is located, as well as close working relationships between IBRD and IFC staff on advisory activities through PEP-MENA, have contributed to an improved country partnership.

Challenges and Opportunities

Though Egypt has undertaken some bold reforms in recent years, there are significant challenges ahead, and IFC can help the country address them.

Challenges

Egypt faces challenges similar to the other middle-income countries (see IEG 2007, appendix E, for a more extensive discussion):

(i) *Continued need for regulatory reform.* Egypt was the top reformer in the 2008 *Doing Business* report, but it needs to sustain the reforms and address the gaps in other areas to tackle constraints on firm growth and improve its current rank of 126.

(ii) *Financial sector reforms.* Competitive financial markets are at the heart of the private sector-led growth process. There is a significant, unfinished agenda in the financial sector, starting with the privatization of the remaining public sector banks. The planned restructuring of the state-owned financial institutions in the nonbank sector is expected to enhance mobilization of savings and improve the allocation of capital. Complementary regulatory and judicial reforms such as setting up specialized economic courts, promoting out-of-court settlement, and enhancing the role of the private credit bureau will also help improve contract enforcement and creditor protection. In turn, this could remove some key obstacles in access to finance of SMEs.

(iii) *Inadequacies in infrastructure.* Removing infrastructure bottlenecks is essential to improving efficiency in production and transport and sustaining high levels of economic growth. Given the huge capital outlays associated with these projects, PPPs have to be developed. The country has some experience with PPPs and can build on them, which could present opportunities for the World Bank Group.

(iv) *Power sector reforms.* The Egyptian authorities are not pursuing IPP project structures for financing the shortfalls in the power sector, contrary to the expectations in this CAS. Instead, they have turned back to the public sector projects to fund new investments in power. In consultation with IBRD, IFC, with its global expertise and experience in handling the difficult projects elsewhere (for example, IPP power projects in Pakistan), may consider advising the government of Egypt on this issue.

(v) *Quality enhancement in advisory services.* In recent years, there has been a rapid expansion of IFC advisory services in Egypt. IFC needs to pay close attention to the results on the ground, verify them judiciously, and learn the lessons as it scales up advisory services operations. The Project Completion Report system, which is being used to capture the results of advisory services operations, needs enhancements to better assess the quality of advisory services engagements.[27]

(vi) *Increased levels of investment.* According to the IMF (IMF 2007), economic growth of around 8 percent per annum will require investment to rise to around 26 percent of GDP (currently at 18 percent). In particular, private sector investments must increase from its low levels of 10 percent (table B.3), which could offer opportunities fo IFC.

Table B.3: Egypt—Economic Indicators, 1999–2006

Indicators	Egypt, Arab Rep. of							
	1999	2000	2001	2002	2003	2004	2005	2006
Private sector								
Gross fixed capital formation, private (% of GDP)	9.9	9.1	9.0	8.4	7.9	7.7	9.1	14.8
Foreign direct investment, net inflows (% of GDP)	1.2	1.2	0.5	0.7	0.3	1.6	6.0	
Private capital flows (% of GDP)	1.8	1.5	2.0	–0.1	0.3	0.9	9.9	
Domestic credit to private sector (% of GDP)	58.7	58.7	62.1	61.9	61.1	54.5	52.2	
Stocks traded, total value (% of GDP)	10.0	11.1	4.0	2.9	4.0	7.1	28.3	44.2
Stocks traded, turnover ratio (%)	31.6	34.7	14.2	16.1	13.7	17.3	43.0	55.2
Market capitalization of listed companies (% of GDP)	36.2	28.8	24.9	29.7	32.6	48.9	88.8	87.0

Indicators	Egypt, Arab Rep. of	Yemen, Rep.	Morocco	Syrian Arab Rep.	Algeria	Tunisia	Indonesia	Turkey	Middle-income countries	Middle East and North Africa
	1999–2006									
Private sector										
Gross fixed capital formation, private (% of GDP)	9.5	13.9	19.9	8.0	14.4	13.3	21.1	13.9	17.9	13.9
Foreign direct investment, net inflows (% of GDP)	1.6	–0.4	1.6	1.1	1.2	2.6	-0.5	1.2	2.9	1.4
Private capital flows (% of GDP)	2.3	–0.4	3.4	1.1		2.6	–0.5	2.9		
Domestic credit to private sector (% of GDP)	58.5	6.3	57.5	9.1	9.9	66.4	22.8	22.8	57.4	39.6
Stocks traded, total value (% of GDP)	13.9		6.4			1.6	10.1	53.5	22.3	6.1
Stocks traded, turnover ratio (%)	28.2		14.0			13.9	42.3	163.3	58.7	17.5
Market capitalization of listed companies (% of GDP)	47.1		42.6			11.6	26.2	36.6	44.4	28.7

Source: World Bank World Development Indicators (September 2007 update).
Note: GDP = gross domestic product.

Table B.4: IFC Investment Operations in Egypt, 1997–2007 ($ '000 and number)

	CAS I					CAS II				CAS III		
Sector	**Fiscal 1997**	**Fiscal 1998**	**Fiscal 1999**	**Fiscal 2000**	**Fiscal 2001**	**Fiscal 2002**	**Fiscal 2003**	**Fiscal 2004**	**Fiscal 2005**	**Fiscal 2006**	**Fiscal 2007**	**Fiscal total**
Agribusiness									15,000	14,000		29,000
									(1)	(1)		(2)
Chemicals	11,972		7,500				10,000				80,000	109,472
	(2)		(1)				(2)				(1)	(6)
Construction			35,000		34,391	31,000		15,000				115,391
and materials			(1)		(1)	(2)		(2)				(6)
Extractive								30,000	1,000	4,280	15,000	50,280
								(1)	(1)	(1)	(1)	(4)
Finance	10,884			3,151	30,000	6,000	30,000	1,947	3,000	48,000	43,521	176,505
	(2)			(2)	(2)	(1)	(1)	(2)	(1)	(4)	(2)	(17)
Funds	5,000											5,000
	(1)											(1)
Health											21,000	21,000
											(2)	(2)
Industrial						4,950					1	4,951
products						(1)					(1)	(2)
Infrastructure					90,000		20,000					110,000
					(2)		(1)					(3)
Metals			71,300									71,300
			(1)									(1)
Pulp and paper		5,000			3,000		353				26,400	34,753
		(1)			(1)		(1)				(1)	(4)
Technical services					2,500							2,500
					(1)							(1)
Textiles								8,000			14,013	22,013
								(1)			(1)	(2)
Tourism	25,589		1,139									26,728
	(2)		(2)									(4)
Trade							15,000				48,500	63,500
							(1)				(1)	(2)
Total	53,445	5,000	114,939	3,151	159,891	41,950	55,353	74,947	19,000	66,280	248,436	842,397
	(7)	(1)	(5)	(2)	(7)	(4)	(5)	(7)	(3)	(6)	(10)	(57)

Source: IFC.
Note: Number of investments is shown in parenthesis.

Table B.5: IFC Advisory Services in Egypt, 1997–2007 ($ '000 and number)

Business line	1998	1999	2000	2001	2002	2004	2005	2006	2007	No info	Total
Access to finance							77	427	845		1,349
							(2)	(4)	(4)		(10)
Business enabling environment		141			24			1,411	644		2,220
		(1)			(1)			(3)	(3)		(8)
Environment and social sustainability			10				374		618		1,002
			(1)				(3)		(1)		(5)
Infrastructure								89	5,186		5,276
								(1)	(6)		(7)
Value addition to firms				75		271		1,033	345	1	1,724
				(1)		(2)		(1)	(1)		(6)
No info	75										75
	(1)										(1)
Total	75	141	10	75	24	271	451	2,960	7,639		11,645
	(1)	(1)	(1)	(1)	(1)	(2)	(5)	(9)	(15)		(37)

Source: IFC.
Note: Number of investments is shown in parentheses.

Table B.6: CAS Priorities and IFC Investment Operations in Egypt, 1997–2007

CAS period	Strategic objectives	IFC priorities identified in CAS	IFC investments
1997–2000	• Export development • Private sector-led growth • Development of human resources • Natural resource management	• Support investments in private and privatizing companies, manufacturing, infrastructure, power, oil and gas, tourism, agribusiness, financial sector	• Cement company (1997) • Red Sea resort (1997) and repeat (rights issue) investments in two Red Sea resorts (1999) • Industrial gases project (1997) • Corrugated boxes manufacturer (1997) • Offshore closed-end fund (1997) • Repeat investment in a carbon black company (1998) • First private joint venture life insurance company in Egypt (2000) • Full-service investment bank (2000)
2001–05	• Reduce poverty and unemployment with a focus on three types of interventions: (i) interventions that support higher and sustained growth; (ii) targeted interventions for poverty reduction; and (iii) interventions with major indirect poverty reduction impacts	• Develop private sector-financed infrastructure • Provide support to the services sector, including tourism • Provide financing to internationally competitive and export-oriented ventures • Support privatization through advisory services to particular transactions and provide financing to privatized ventures • Support SMEs • Develop financial markets • Possibly participate in building pipelines to export Egypt's large natural gas reserves to Eastern Mediterranean countries	• Two power sector (IPP) investments (2001) • Repeat investments in a corrugated boxes manufacturer (2001, 2003) • IT consulting company (2001) • Commercial bank (2001) • Repeat investment in a cement company (2001) • A leading investment bank (2001) • One of the first leasing companies in Egypt (2002) • Export-oriented motor vehicle parts company (2002) • Ceramic sanitary ware company (2002) • IFC's first partial guarantee of a cross-border private placement of debt in the Middle East and North Africa Region, in support of a leading Egyptian conglomerate (2002) • Repeat investment in a carbon black company (2003) • Grocery store (2003) • Organic produce and medicines manufacturer (2003) • Egypt trade facility (2003) • First private specialized housing finance company (2004) • First fully private port in Egypt (2004) • Two investments in Egypt's leading sanitary ware company (2004) • Life insurance company rights issue (2004) • First North African acrylic fiber plant (2004) • Natural gas development (2004) • Leading Egyptian poultry group (2005) • First factoring company in Egypt (2005) • Interest rate swap for an existing oil and gas company (2005)
2006–09	• Facilitating private sector development • Enhancing the provision of public services • Promoting equity	*Investment operations:* • Support PPI initiatives with guarantee, capital, or advisory services • Assist in the development of new financial sector institutions and instruments for the private sector • Catalyze new private sector investment in manufacturing,	• Coca-Cola bottler (2006) • Metal ore mining (2006) • Repeat investment in Egypt's largest investment bank (2006) • Bank privatization of the second largest bank in the country (2006) • Commercial bank (2006) • Repeat investment in a leasing company (2006) • Investment in a small, family-owned oil & gas company (2007) • Health care provider (2007) • Phosphatic fertilizer producer (2007)

(*Continued on the following page*)

Table B.6: CAS Priorities and IFC Investment Operations in Egypt, 1997–2007 (*continued*)

CAS period	Strategic objectives	IFC priorities identified in CAS	IFC investments
		petrochemicals, oil and gas, and the social sectors • Support SME initiatives *Advisory services:* • PEP-MENA expected to be the main vehicle within the five technical assistance pillars for the financial sector, support to SMEs, assistance for improvement of the business enabling environment, support for the development of public-private partnerships (particularly for infrastructure), and assistance in privatizing or restructuring state-owned enterprises. • Facilitate cross-border investments into Egypt and support expansion of the internationally competitive Egyptian companies into new markets (South-South investments) • Explore the scope for private participation in the power distribution subsector and develop alternative sources for generation such as wind power.	• Mortgage finance (2007) • Paper tissue manufacturer expanding regionally (2007) • Rights issue investment for restructuring a compressor manufacturer (2007) • Grocery store chain (2007) • Hospital group expanding regionally (2007) • "Home textiles" company (2007) • Commercial bank expanding regionally (2007) • Repeat investment in a poultry group (2007)

Source: IFC.
Note: IPP = independent power producer; PEP-MENA = Private Enterprise Partnership for the Middle East and North Africa; PPI = private participation in infrastructure; SME = small- and medium-size enterprise.

Government

Ministry of Investment

Minister H.E., Dr. Mahmoud Mohieldin
Advisor to Minister, Mona A. Zobaa
Advisor to Minister, Mohamed S. Hassouna

Ministry of International Cooperation

Minister H.E., Fayza Aboul Naga
Former Undersecretary, Dr. Ahmed El Darsh
Desk Officer Cooperation with Regional and Intern. Organ., Noran Aly Kamel
Second Secretary Minister's Office, Walid El Melegy
Assistant to the Minister, Mostafa Ismail Abdel Latif
Director General, International Organizations, Fatma Amin
Director General, International Finance Organizations, Seham Abdel Baky

Ministry of Finance

Former Minister of Finance, Dr. Medhat Hassanein
Advisor to Minister, Mumtaz el Saeed
Advisor to Minister, Hisham Tawfik
General Manager, Ali Abdellatif
Head of Large Taxpayer Center, Seif Coutry

Ministry of Industry and Trade

Advisor, Prof. Mona El Garf
Focal Point for TVET Reform, Hala El Shawarby
Skills Development Project Director, Eng. Nihal Abdel Hamid

Ministry of Water Resources and Irrigation

Minister H.E., Mahmoud Abou Zeid
Undersecretary of State, Dr. Mohammed Bahaa El Din
Minister's Office, Director for Research & Special Studies, Dr. Essam Khalifa
Advisor to Director for Research & Special Studies, Eng. Ahmad Abde Aziz
Chairman Mechanical & Electric Department, Eng. Sami Ouf
Advisor to Minister, Dr. Safwat Abdel Dayem
IIIMP Coordinator, Dr. Fatma Abdel Rahman
Head Minister's Technical Office Sector, Dr. Hussein El-Atfy
Chairman, Egyptian Public Authority for Drainage Projects (EPADP), Reda El Bendary
Advisor to Chairman, Eng. Wedad Khalaf
Head, Planning Sector, Eng. Adel Khafaga
Head, Horizontal Expansion Projects Sector, Eng. Ibrahim Harshash
Head, Irrigation Improvement Sector, Eng. Fawzi El Abd
Deputy PMU Director, Sohag project, Eng. Mounir Hosney

Water projects

Deputy Chief M&E, (EPADP), Aly Saeed
Director Information Systems, Samia Kamal
National Drainage, Umamiah Shaeen
Consultant, Wicher Boissevain
Integrated Irrigation, Dr. Fatmah Attia
West Delta, Safwat Abdel Dayeim
Irrigation Improvement, Adel Madbouly
Pumping Station III, Mahmoud Aboul Fatouh

Ministry of Electricity and Energy

Minister H.E., Hassan Younnes
Undersecretary of State, Aktham AbouEl Ella
Executive Chairman, Samir Hassan

Ministry of Civil Aviation

Minister H.E., Ahmed Shafik
Chief of Financial Sector, Youssri Amir

Head of Planning Sector, Mohamed Tobar
PMU Director, Magda Moussa

Ministry of State for Environment
EPAP 2 PMU Deputy Director, Maysoon Ali
Technical Support Team Manager, Eng. Yasser Askar
Eng. Hanna Gomaa
Eng. Ahmed Medhat

Ministry of Education
First Undersecretary General Education, Dr. Reda Abou Serie
First Undersecretary Technical Education, Dr. N.A. Aziz Mohmoud
Undersecretary Secondary Education, Wagdy Afify
Advisor to Minister, Dr. Hassan Billawy
EEP/SEEP PMU Director, Dr. Mostafa A. Samie

Ministry of Higher Education
Minister H.E., Hani Helal
PMU Executive Director, Dr. Mohsen El Mahdy Said

Ministry of Health and Population
First Undersecretary (Curative), Prof. Dr. Nasser Rasmi
DG & Health Insurance Coordinator, Dr. Hala Massekh
Head, Central Dept. Tech. Support & Projects, Dr. Emam Moussa
Manager HSRP Dept of Projects, Dr. Osama Hassan Abd El Azim
McKinsey Consultant, Tim Knapp

Central Bank
Deputy Governor, Tarek Amer
Assistant Sub-Governor, Lobna Helal
Division Chief, Rania Al-Mashat

Social Fund for Development
Director Gen. Proj. & Specialized Units, Mohamed Hashem
Head, Community Development Dept., Medhat Massoud
Manager, Int'l. Coop Group, Aliaa El Sherif
Sr. Officer, Int'l. Coop Group, Ahmed Farag

Egyptian Environmental Affairs Agency
Advisor to the Minister, Mohammed Sayed Khalil
Director Conservation Sector, Prof. Moustafa Fouda
Head of Environment Management, Fatma Abou Shouk

General Authority for Government Services
Chairman, Mohamed El Far
Public Procurement Specialist, Mohamed Atta
Public Procurement Specialist, Gamalat Talaak

Mortgage Finance Authority
Chairman, Osama Saleh
Deputy Chairman, Ashraf El-Kady

Insurance Supervisory Authority
Deputy, Yehia Abdel Ghafar

General Authority for Investment and Free Zones
Chairman, Ziad Bahaa Eldin
Vice Chairman, Neveen El Shafei

Egyptian Holding Company for Airports and Air Navigation
Chairman, Holding Co., Ibrahim Manaa
Engineer, Ibrahim Ahmed Manaa

Egyptian Airports Co.
Chairman, Magdeldin Refaat

Egyptian Electricity Holding Co.
Chairman, Mohamed Awad
Executive Director, Kamel Yassin

Power Generation Engineering and Services Company
Project Control Manager, Mohsen Teama
Projects Manager, Said Ahmed
Projects Control Engineer, Kareem Bakar

Field Trip to Delta
Director Irrigation project, Ahmed Hamad
EPADP, Eng. Mahmoud El-Tahib
EPADP, Eng. Tarek Adbel-Aziz
EPADP, Eng. Abdel-Al Mohamdie Nasef

Irrigation Service, Eng. Mohammed Mahsoud
Irrigation Improvement Sector, Eng. Kafr El Shiekh
Irrigation Improvement Sector, Adel Abdel-Aziz

Private Sector

Arab African International Bank
Deputy Chairman, Hasan Abdalla

Bank Misr
Deputy Chairman, Mohamed Ozalp
General Manager, Effat Ishak
Consultant, Change & Restructuring, A.E. Zidan

Bank of Alexandria
Chairman, Mahmood Abdel Latif

National Bank of Egypt
Deputy Chairman, Attia Salem
General Research Manager, Salwa El-Antary

Commercial Investment Bank
Chairman & Managing Director, Hisham Ezz El-Arab

Tourism Development Authority
Former Director, Dr. Adel Rady
Sr. Technical Advisor, Dr. Nabil Saba

Soma Bay Development Company
Director, Dr. Farid Saad
Financial Controller, Noman Hakim

Civil Society and Academics

Egypt Center for Economic Studies
Director, Hanaa Kheir-el-Din

Economic Research Forum
Managing Director, Dr. Ahmed Galal
Lead Author HDR 07, Dr. Heba Handoussa

The Center for Environment and Development for the Arab Region and Europe (CEDARE)
Program Manager, Dr. Khaled Abou Zeid

Kreditanstalt für Wiederaufbau – Cairo
Director, Andreas Holtkotte
Water and Environment Sr. Programme Officer, Walid M. Abdel-Rehim

National Council of Women
Secretary General H.E., Farkhonda Hassan

Donors

USAID
Former Mission Director, Hank Bassford
Former Mission Director, Ken Ellis
Former Associate Director, Jim Norris
Associate Mission Director, Joseph S. Ryan
Former Mission Project Manager, Amal Mowafy
Water Resource Specialist, Eng. Wafaa Faltaous
Red Sea Project Manager, Halla Hassenein
Health Head, Holly Dempsey
Education Advisor, Adel Gohar
Education Advisor, Hala El Serafy
Sr. Economist, Mark Gellerson
Sr. Economic Advisor, Ali Kamel
Chief of Party, TAPR II Contract, Richard Laliberte
Sr. Economist, Policy and Private Sector Office, Ingi Lotfi
Former Deputy Director, Mary Ott
Economic Specialist, Policy and Private Sector Office, Mervat Fikry Sidra
Advisor on Policy Reform, Than Truong
Sr. Education Advisor, Elizabeth Warfield

African Development Bank
Resident Representative, Omar Aw
Country Operations Officer, Almaz Amine
Procurement Advisor, Ashraf Ayad

International Monetary Fund
Senior Resident Representative, Cyrus Sassanpour
Mission Chief, Klaus Enders
Fiscal Affairs Department, Aliona Cebotari
Fiscal Affairs Department, Isaias Coelho

Food and Agriculture Organization of the United Nations

Sr. Irrigation and Water Resources Officer, Mohamed Bazza

Associate Professional Officer, Regional Policy Assistance, Lise Albrechsten

Associate Professional Officer, Regional Policy Assistance, Maurice Saade

European Union

Horizontal Issues Advisor, Enrico Barisonzi

Counselor, Nicola Bellomo

Project Manager for Basic Education, Sylvia Crescimbeni

Save the Children UK

Social Protection & Advocacy Adviser, Dr. Alaa Sebeh

World Food Program

Egypt Country Director, Bishow B. Parajuli

United Nations Development Programme

Country Director, Mounir Tabet

GTZ

Egypt Country Director, Marlis Weissenborn

Netherland Embassy

Sr. Program Officer, Drinking Water Sanitation, Tarek Morad

APPENDIX D: GUIDE TO IEG'S COUNTRY ASSISTANCE EVALUATION METHODOLOGY

This methodological note describes the key elements of the Independent Evaluation Group–World Bank's (IEG–WB's) Country Assistance Evaluation (CAE) methodology.[1]

CAEs rate the outcomes of Bank assistance programs, not the clients' overall development progress.

A Bank assistance program needs to be assessed on how well it met its particular objectives, which are typically a subset of the client's development objectives. If a Bank assistance program is large in relation to the client's total development effort, the program outcome will be similar to the client's overall development progress. However, most Bank assistance programs provide only a fraction of the total resources devoted to a client's development by donors, stakeholders, and the government itself. In CAEs, IEG rates only the outcome of the Bank's program, not the client's overall development outcome, although the latter is clearly relevant for judging the program's outcome.

The experience gained in CAEs confirms that Bank program outcomes sometimes diverge significantly from the client's overall development progress. CAEs have identified Bank assistance programs that had—

- Satisfactory outcomes matched by good client development
- Unsatisfactory outcomes in clients that achieved good overall development results, notwithstanding the weak Bank program
- Satisfactory outcomes in clients that did not achieve satisfactory overall results during the period of program implementation.

Assessments of assistance program outcome and Bank performance are not the same.

By the same token, an unsatisfactory Bank assistance program outcome does not always mean that Bank performance was also unsatisfactory, and vice versa. This becomes clearer once we consider that the Bank's contribution to the outcome of its assistance program is only part of the story. The assistance program's outcome is determined by the *joint* impact of four agents: (i) the client, (ii) the Bank, (iii) partners and other stakeholders, and (iv) exogenous forces (for example, events of nature, international economic shocks, and so forth). Under the right circumstances, a negative contribution from any one agent might overwhelm the positive contributions from the other three and lead to an unsatisfactory outcome.

IEG–WB measures Bank performance primarily on the basis of contributory actions the Bank directly controlled. Judgments regarding Bank performance typically consider the relevance and implementation of the strategy; the design and supervision of the Bank's lending interventions; the scope, quality, and follow-up of diagnostic work and other analytical and advisory assistance activities; the consistency of the Bank's lending with its nonlending work and with its safeguard policies; and the Bank's partnership activities.

Rating Assistance Program Outcome

In rating the outcome (expected development impact) of an assistance program, IEG–WB gauges the extent to which major strategic objectives were relevant and achieved, without any shortcomings. In other words, did the Bank do the right thing, and did it do it right?

Programs typically express their goals in terms of higher-order objectives, such as poverty reduction. The Country Assistance Strategy (CAS) may also establish intermediate goals, such as improved targeting of social services or promotion of integrated rural development, and specify how they are expected to contribute toward achieving the higher-order objective. IEG–WB's task is then to validate whether the intermediate objectives were the right ones, whether they produced satisfactory net benefits, and whether the results chain specified in the CAS was valid. Where causal linkages were not fully specified in the CAS, it is the evaluator's task to reconstruct this causal chain from the available evidence and assess relevance, efficacy, and outcome with reference to the intermediate and higher-order objectives.

For each of the main objectives, the CAE evaluates the relevance of the objective; the relevance of the Bank's strategy toward meeting the objective, including the balance between lending and nonlending instruments; and the efficacy with which the strategy was implemented and the results achieved. This is done in two steps. The first is a top-down review of whether the Bank program achieved a particular Bank objective or planned outcome and had a substantive impact on the country's development. The second step is a bottom-up review of the Bank products and services (lending, analytical and advisory services, and aid coordination) used to achieve the objective. Together these two steps test the consistency of findings from the products and services and the development impact dimensions. Subsequently, an assessment is made of the relative contribution to the results achieved by the Bank, other donors, and the government, as well as exogenous factors.

Evaluators also assess the degree of client ownership of international development priorities, such as the Millennium Development Goals, and Bank corporate advocacy priorities, such as safeguards. Ideally, any differences in dealing with these issues would be identified and resolved by the CAS, enabling the evaluator to focus on whether the trade-offs adopted were appropriate. However, in other instances, the strategy may be found to have glossed over certain conflicts or avoided addressing key client development constraints. In either case, the consequences could include a diminution of program relevance, a loss of client ownership, and/or unwelcome side effects, such as safeguard violations, all of which must be taken into account in judging program outcome.

Ratings scale

IEG–WB utilizes six rating categories for **outcome,** ranging from highly satisfactory to highly unsatisfactory (see box D.1).

The **institutional development impact** can be rated as *high, substantial, modest, or negligible*. Institutional development impact measures the extent to which the program bolstered the client's ability to make more efficient, equitable, and sustainable use of its human, financial, and natural resources. Examples of areas included in judging the institutional development impact of the program are—

- The soundness of economic management
- The structure of the public sector and, in particular, the civil service
- The institutional soundness of the financial sector
- The soundness of legal, regulatory, and judicial systems
- The extent of monitoring and evaluation systems
- The effectiveness of aid coordination
- The degree of financial accountability
- The extent of building nongovernmental organization capacity
- The level of social and environmental capital.

Sustainability can be rated as *highly likely, likely, unlikely, highly unlikely*, or, if available information is insufficient, *nonevaluable*. Sustainability measures the resilience to risk of the development benefits of the country assistance program over time, taking into account eight factors:

Box D.1: Ratings Scale

Highly satisfactory	The assistance program achieved at least acceptable progress toward all major relevant objectives and had best practice development impact on one or more of them. No major shortcomings were identified.
Satisfactory	The assistance program achieved acceptable progress toward all major relevant objectives. No best practice achievements or major shortcomings were identified.
Moderately satisfactory	The assistance program achieved acceptable progress toward most of its major relevant objectives. No major shortcomings were identified.
Moderately unsatisfactory	The assistance program did not make acceptable progress toward most of its major relevant objectives, or it made acceptable progress on all of them, but either (i) did not take into adequate account a key development constraint or (ii) produced a major shortcoming, such as a safeguard violation.
Unsatisfactory	The assistance program did not make acceptable progress toward most of its major relevant objectives and either (i) did not take into adequate account a key development constraint or (ii) produced a major shortcoming, such as a safeguard violation.
Highly unsatisfactory	The assistance program did not make acceptable progress toward any of its major relevant objectives and did not take into adequate account a key development constraint, while also producing at least one major shortcoming, such as a safeguard violation.

- Technical resilience
- Financial resilience (including policies on cost recovery)
- Economic resilience
- Social support (including conditions subject to safeguard policies)
- Environmental resilience
- Ownership by governments and other key stakeholders
- Institutional support (including a supportive legal/regulatory framework, and organizational and management effectiveness)
- Resilience to exogenous effects, such as international economic shocks or changes in the political and security environments.

A successfully completed irrigation project; 97 percent of the population in Egypt lives near the Nile River, so irrigation is crucial.
Photo by Ray Witlin, courtesy of the World Bank Photo Library.

Ministry of International Cooperation
The Minister

June 8th, 2008

Dear Mr. Gray,

Reference to your letter dated May 15th, 2008 regarding the Egypt-Country Assistance Evaluation draft report that was prepared by the Independent Evaluation Group(IEG), I would first like to commend the IEG for its efforts in preparing such a comprehensive and precise report and express my consensus with all of the report's very important recommendations especially those concerning future efforts for the reduction of poverty rates and income discrepancies, human development and focus on the environmental, social and infrastructure sectors. Nevertheless, I would like to put emphasis on the extreme importance and urgency of the report's recommendation to include a much more "flexible lending program" that takes into account Egypt's status as a Middle Income Country. Even though this has already started with the New IBRD's Lending Strategy to the MICs , yet -while we really appreciate this step- we consider it only as a first step and more must follow in this track. This is because still most MICs still can not afford to borrow at IBRD rates especially when they tend to finance projects with social dimensions (like those in the health and education sectors) that don't create enough revenues for the loans repayment. The GOE has suggested in many of our dialogues the establishment of a special window at the bank to provide concessional lending to MICs. This could be in the form of loans to finance such projects as well as grants to finance projects preparation and provide technical assistance.

Ministry of International Cooperation
The Minister

Furthermore, I would like to point out that the World Bank should be more of a knowledge-Institution than a financial one; and thus should share its international experiences with Egypt and provide it with best practices especially for debt-servicing, financial and social reform, building good governance and adopting anti-corruption measures.

I hope that the World Bank - as one of Egypt's most essential development partners - would tackle these recommendations with a sense of urgency and necessity by starting at once its work with the Egyptian Government to develop concrete action plans in this regard. Finally, I would like to pay tribute to the World Bank for becoming more and more responsive to Egypt's development priorities and wish it would continue moving in this trend. Please accept, Mr. Gray, my best regards.

Sincerely,
Fayza Aboulnaga

Minister of International Cooperation

Mr. Cheryl W.Gray
Director
Independent Evaluation Group
World Bank

Chapter 3

1. After the end of the review period, the government launched a three-year program to phase out most industrial energy subsidies. But prices for most energy products are still far below world prices.

2. One of the government's arguments for not doing a complete PER is that it wanted quick gains in the form of savings in the major spending sectors, such as health and education. A full PER would have taken longer and probably would have not provided the specific measures the government needed. However, the PER notes do not allow an analysis of the trade-offs of budget allocation across sectors. The first fiscal note focused on the construction of the budget, highlighting the lack of fiscal transparency and the lack of expenditure prioritization. The second focused on budget execution, with special emphasis on fiscal decentralization. It offered policy actions for decentralizing expenditure, revenue, debt, and performance monitoring. The third note focused on fiscal and public debt sustainability.

3. This standard helps guide members that have or that might seek access to international capital markets in the provision of their economic and financial data to the public.

4. Between 2004 and 2006, the number of inspections per year for manufacturing companies fell from an average of nearly 30 per firm to 20, a number that is low relative to regional comparators.

5. Mortgage issues also support the Growth Pole projects planned in major areas.

Chapter 4

1. In 2000, passenger traffic peaked at 8.9 million at Cairo International Airport, with a maximum rated capacity of 9 million passengers. An expansion in the airport was necessary to absorb additional traffic without a rapid deterioration of service. This was especially critical because 76 percent of passengers were international. Tourism has been the country's second largest earner of foreign exchange, after hydrocarbons, and it has been the main employer of the private sector. The country's other airports, which primarily serve tourism, experienced average growth rates of nearly 13 percent per year between 1993 and 2002. Of these airports, Sharm El Sheikh, which grew the fastest, was handling the second largest tourist traffic in Egypt. Airport capacity nationwide increasingly was becoming too small and the government was giving a high priority to an airport expansion program. The government also initiated sweeping civil aviation sector reforms in 2001. The Ministry of Civil Aviation was created in 2002 and entrusted with overall responsibility for the country's airports and civil aviation matters.

Chapter 5

1. Gross enrollment ratio is the ratio of total enrollment, regardless of age, to the population of the group that officially corresponds to the level of education shown. It indicates the capacity of each level of the educational system. Overage or underage enrollments to primary education frequently occur for cultural or economic reasons. It is also important to consider repetition rates. These rates are quite high in some developing countries, leading to a substantial number of overage children enrolled in each grade and thus raising the gross enrollment ratio. The gross enrollment ratio in primary school can be higher than 100 percent for these reasons.

Appendix B

1. Most of the analysis in this Country Evaluation Note is for the 1999–2007 period, following the time frame for IEG–WB's CAE. However, for the analysis of the CASs, it uses the 1997–2007 period, as the CAS I started in 1997.

2. This appendix was prepared by Cherian Samuel, Evaluation Officer, and Izlem Yenice, Evaluation Analyst, under the direction of Stoyan Tenev, Head, Macro Evaluation, and Amitava Banerjee, Manager, IEG–IFC.

3. Based on 2006 GNI per capita, lower-middle-income countries range from $906 to $3,595 and higher-middle-income countries, $3,596 to $11,115.

4. Between 1999 and 2006, GDP growth rate was 4.6 percent per annum, slightly above the Region average of 4 percent, but below the 5.2 percent for all middle-income countries. Though the review period started with a high GDP growth of 6.1 percent in 1999, the economy was in a recession from 2001 to 2003, when the per capita GDP growth was barely 1 percent per annum.

5. See World Bank (2006b). The reforms included (i) restructuring and slashing customs duties; (ii) improving management of exchange rate and monetary policies; (iii) accelerating the privatization program (sale proceeds of $32.2 billion or 4 percent of GDP since June 2004, which exceeded expectations); (iv) advancing fiscal reforms with drastically reduced personal and corporate tax rates and simplified tax structure; (v) substantially limiting regulatory impediments to business entry and licensing; (vi) partially adjusting prices for some fuel products; and (vii) concluding new trade agreements.

6. Egypt's Institutional Investor Country Credit Rating score improved from 44.9 in 1999 to 49.8 in 2007 and the Heritage Index from 58.6 in 1999 to 53.2 in 2007.

7. These were followed by factor market issues (finance, labor skills, regulation, and land). See World Bank (2005e) for more details. These findings are also consistent with the World Economic Forum's Competitiveness Report for 2006–07, according to which the three most problematic factors for doing business in Egypt are access to financing, inefficient government bureaucracy, and an inadequately educated workforce.

8. An IFC investee.

9. According to United Nations Conference on Trade and Development figures, net FDI inflows increased from $509.4 million (0.5 percent of GDP) in fiscal 2000–01 to $6.1 billion (8.5 percent of GDP) in fiscal 2005–06 and $11.1 billion in fiscal 2006–07.

10. Egypt's stock exchange posted the world's highest returns on its local market index in 2005. The Egyptian local index more than doubled for the second year a row, gaining 155 percent in dollar terms. Egypt has Africa's second-largest bourse, after South Africa. See Oxford Analytica (2006) for more details.

11. According to the 2005 CAS, micro and small and medium enterprises are a significant force in the Egyptian economy. Enterprises with fewer than 10 workers are estimated to contribute 80 percent of private sector value added and account for 75 percent of employment. See World Bank (2005b, p. 91).

12. Data presented in table B.3 show that Egyptian firms in the investment climate assessment used only 7 percent of bank financing for investment, compared to 17 percent for the Region and 15 percent for all countries. In contrast, the share of internal finance for Egyptian firms was 86 percent, significantly above the 67 percent for the Region and 58 percent for all countries.

13. The state fully owns the three largest commercial banks (National Bank of Egypt, Banque Misr, and Banque du Caire) and three specialized banks (Egyptian Arab Land Bank, Industrial Development Bank of Egypt, and Principal Bank for Development and Agricultural Credit). A fourth one, Bank of Alexandria, was sold in December 2006 to an Italian bank, São Paolo, which acquired an 80 percent share for $1.6 billion. Banque du Caire is slated for privatization this year. Banking sector consolidation is on track, with the number of banks reduced from 57 in 2004 to 43 in 2007. Public sector banks also owned equity capital—and de facto government sway—in 17 joint venture banks, most of which were privatized during 2004–06.

14. Dobranogov and Iqbal (2005). About four-fifths (80 percent) of the Egypt's domestic debt in 2003 was instrumented through T-bills with 3- to 12-month maturity, and some three-quarters of domestic debt was held by government-owned banks.

15. Asset possession is also a major issue, especially when it comes to targeting small and medium-size enterprises.

These are all the advisory services assignments for which IFC could find information and therefore excludes some earlier operations. Of the 36 advisory services operations, 27 (75 percent) were approved between 2005 and 2007.

In terms of results, 14 (39 percent by number and 18 percent by amount) of the 36 advisory services operations have a project completion report/technical advisory services (PCR/TAS) completion report, with most others being too new, with results "too early to tell." In general, advisory service operations were not linked to specific IFC investments, except for two in mortgage finance. The PCR/TAS completion reports were of varying quality, with most lacking appropriate baseline data. Also, some of the project completion reports did not routinely report on all project components; it was not always clear whether the components had been dropped or had simply been ignored or overlooked in tracking and evaluation.

16. Commitments range from a low of $3.1 million in fiscal 2000 to $248 million in 2007.

17. The first set of IFC power sector investments were IPPs. However, Egyptian authorities developed mistrust of the IPP structures over time and have turned back to the public sector for meeting the country's power needs.

18. Of the 57 committed investments, eight—five rights issues, one restructuring, and two swaps—have to be excluded for Expanded Project Supervision Report (XPSR) evaluation purposes, leaving a total of 49. However, given the five-year lag between approvals/commitments and evaluation, not all 49 investments need to be considered in the current analysis. It is sufficient to consider the investments evaluated between 2002 and 2007—committed between 1997 and 2002—which turns out to be 19. Of these 19 investments, 8 have been subject to XPSR evaluations and another 5 have Development Outcome Tracking System ratings. IEG does not undertake mini-XPSR reviews for Country Evaluation Notes, like this review of Egypt. Among the eight investments with XPSRs, three were rated as successful in terms of Development Objective and Internal Order ratings. Likewise, of the five other investments with Development Outcome Tracking System ratings, four were rated as successful.

19. These are all the advisory services assignments for which IFC could find some information and therefore excludes some earlier operations. Of the 36 advisory services operations, 27 (75 percent) were approved between 2005 and 2007.

20. In terms of results, 14 (39 percent by number and 18 percent by amount) of the 36 advisory services operations have a PCR/TAS report, with most others being too new, with results "too early to tell." In general, advisory service operations were not linked to specific IFC investments, except for two in mortgage finance. The PCR/TAS completion reports were of varying qualities, with most lacking appropriate baseline data. Also, some of the project completion reports did not routinely report on all project components; it was not always clear whether the components had been dropped or had simply been ignored or overlooked in tracking and evaluation.

21. This seems to be consistent with the high share of the Egyptian manufacturing sector in GDP (18.6 percent), compared with the Region's average of 12.6 percent, but a little lower than the middle-income countries' average of 22 percent. But the share of industry in GDP for Egypt is 34 percent, which is similar to the middle-income country average of 35.9 percent, but lower than the Region's average of 41.7 percent. The high industry share of the Region reflects the importance of the oil and gas sector for those countries.

22. IFC credit lines to Egyptian commercial banks for on-lending to small and medium-size enterprises have been few. IFC committed two loans in 2001 and 2006 to a leasing company for on-lending to small and medium-size enterprises. It has also provided technical assistance to commercial banks to downscale.

23. The average loan and equity credit risk review ratings were 3 and 4, respectively. Of the 25 investments committed after 2002 with credit risk review ratings, only one investment had a poor loan/equity (CRR) rating, 5 and above.

24. Export development was a strategic objective during the CAS I period as well, and IFC support became operative with a lag, during the second CAS period.

25. Based on the IEG-IFC case study of Egypt, as part of the IEG work on Bank-IFC collaboration in middle-income countries.

26. IFC's Cairo office was set up in 1978 and its Middle East and North Africa director moved there in 1999.

27. These findings are based on IEG's validation of Pilot II project completion reports in Egypt, which are consistent with findings from other project completion reports as well.

Appendix D

1. In this note, *assistance program* refers to products and services generated in support of the economic development of a client country over a specified period of time, and *client* refers to the country that receives the benefits of that program.

The World Bank's Airport Development Project is the largest Bank project in the Middle East and North Africa Region, doubling the capacity of passenger terminals at two airports. Such projects will facilitate Egypt's rising tourism industry. Photo courtesy of Victor Orozco, World Bank Group.

Allaoua, Zoubida. 2005. "Dynamizing the Investment Climate in MENA: Benchmarking Constraints and Expanding Opportunity and Employment." Presentation, December 4–6, Cairo. http:go.worldbank.org/00H8VL5FH0.

Billmeier, Andreas, and Isabella Massa. 2007. "Go Long or Short in Pyramids? News from the Egyptian Stock Market." IMF Working Paper WP/07/179, International Monetary Fund, Washington, DC.

Dobranogov, Anton, and Farrukh Iqbal. 2005. "Economic Growth in Egypt: Constraints and Determinants." Middle East and North Africa Working Paper Series No. 42, World Bank, Washington, DC.

Eberhard, Anton, and Katharine Nawaal Gratwick. 2007. "From State to Market and Bank Again: Egypt's Experiment with Independent Power Projects." *The Energy Journal,* 32: 724–38.

Economic Consulting Associates. 2007. *Egypt: Economic Costs of Natural Gas.* London: ECA Ltd.

FAO (Food and Agricultural Organization). 2005. "Irrigation in Africa in Figures: AWUASTAT Survey—2005." FAO Water Report No. 29, Food and Agriculture Organization of the United Nations, Rome.

Galal, Ahmed, and Nadeem Ul Haque, eds. 2006. *Fiscal Sustainability in Emerging Markets—International Experience and Implications for Egypt*. Cairo, Egypt: The American University in Cairo Press.

Ikram, Khalid. 2006. *The Egyptian Economy 1952–2000—Performance, Policies, and Issues*. New York: Routledge.

IEG (Independent Evaluation Group). 2008a. *Environmental Sustainability: An Evaluation of World Bank Group Support.* IEG Study Series. Washington, DC: World Bank.

———. 2008b. *Public Sector Reform: What Works and Why? An IEG Evaluation of World Bank Support.* IEG Study Series. Washington, DC: World Bank.

———. 2007. *Development Results in Middle-Income Countries: An Evaluation of the World Bank's Support.* IEG Study Series. Washington, DC: World Bank.

———. 2006. "Arab Republic of Egypt: Client Perspectives on Elements of World Bank Support." Working Paper No. 41120, World Bank, Washington, DC.

———. 2002. *Social Funds: Assessing Effectiveness.* IEG Study Series. Washington, DC: World Bank.

———. 2000. "Egypt Country Assistance Evaluation." Report No. 20513, World Bank, Washington, DC.

IMF (International Monetary Fund). 2007. "Arab Republic of Egypt—2007 Article IV Consultation. Preliminary Conclusions of the IMF Mission." http://www.imf.org/external/np/ms/2007/091207.htm.

———. 2006a. *Direction of Trade Statistics Yearbook.* Washington, DC: IMF.

———. 2006b. "Statement by the IMF Mission on the 2006 Article IV Consultation with the Arab Republic of Egypt." http://www.imf.org/external/np/sec/pr/2006.pr0674.htm.

———. 2005. "Arab Republic of Egypt: 2005 Article IV Consultation—Staff Report; Public Information Notice on the Executive Board Discussion; and Statement by the Executive Director for the Arab Republic of Egypt." IMF Country Report No. 05/177, IMF, Washington, DC.

———. 1998. "Egypt: Beyond Stabilization, Toward a Dynamic Market Economy." Occasional Paper No. 163, IMF, Washington, DC.

Nassar, Heba. 2003. "The Economics of Tobacco in Egypt: A New Analysis of Demand." HNP Discussion Paper, Economics of Tobacco Control Paper No. 8, World Health Organization and World Bank, Geneva and Washington, DC.

OECD (Organisation for Economic Co-operation and Development). 2007. *Egypt: OECD Investment Policy Reviews.* Paris: OECD.

Oxford Analytica. 2006. "Africa: Stock Markets Face Limited Growth Prospects." February 23.

UNCTAD (United Nations Conference on Trade and Development). 2007. *World Investment Report 2007: Transnational Corporations, Extractive Industries, and Development.* New York and Geneva: United Nations.

UNDP (United Nations Development Programme). 2005. *Egypt Human Development Report 2005—Choosing our Future: Towards a New Social Contract.* New York and Cairo, Egypt: UNDP and Institute of National Planning, Egypt.

Vedavalli, Rangaswamy. 2007. *Energy for Development—Twenty-First Century Challenges of Reform and Liberalization in Developing Countries*. New York: Anthem.

World Bank. 2008a. "Access to Finance and Economic Growth in Egypt." Report No. 41305, World Bank, Washington, DC.

———. 2008b. *Doing Business 2008.* Washington, DC: World Bank.

———. 2007a. "Arab Republic of Egypt: A Poverty Assessment Update." Report No. 39885-EGT, World Bank, Washington, DC.

———. 2007b. "Export Diversification in Egypt, Jordan, Lebanon, Morocco, and Tunisia." Report No. 40497-MNA, World Bank, Washington, DC.

———. 2006a. "Egypt: Health Policy Note." Egypt Public Expenditure Review, Report No. 46938, World Bank, Washington, DC.

———. 2006b. "Program Document for a Proposed Loan in the Amount of US$500 Million Equivalent to the Arab Republic of Egypt for a Financial Development Policy Loan." Report No. 36197-EG, World Bank, Washington, DC.

———. 2005a. "Arab Republic of Egypt Country Environmental Analysis (1992–2002)." World Bank, Washington, DC.

———. 2005b. "Egypt: Country Assistance Strategy for Arab Republic of Egypt for the Period FY06–FY09." Report No. 32190-EG, World Bank, Washington, DC.

———. 2005c. "Egypt and the Millennium Development Goals: Challenges and Opportunities." HNP Discussion Paper, World Bank, Washington, DC.

———. 2005d. "Egypt: Toward a More Effective Social Policy—Subsidies and Social Safety Net." Background Paper, Report No. 33550-EG, World Bank, Washington, DC.

———. 2005e. "Egypt: Towards a Better Investment Climate for Growth and Employment Creation." Private Sector, Financial Sector, and Infrastructure Group Report No. 36675, World Bank, Washington, DC.

———. 2004. "Arab Republic of Egypt: Poverty Reduction Strategy for Egypt." Report No. 27954-EGT, World Bank, Washington, DC, and Ministry of Planning, Government of the Arab Republic of Egypt.

———. 2003. "Arab Republic of Egypt: Strategic Options for Early Childhood Education." Report No. 24772-EGT, World Bank, Washington, DC.

———. 2002a. "Arab Republic of Egypt: Cost Assessment of Environmental Degradation." Sector Note, Report No. 25175-EGT, World Bank, Washington, DC.

———. 2002b. "Arab Republic of Egypt Education Sector Review: Progress and Priorities for the Future." Report No. 24905-EGT, World Bank, Washington, DC.

———. 2002c. "Egypt: Poverty Reduction in Egypt—Diagnosis and Strategy." Sector Report No. 24234, World Bank, Washington, DC.

———. 2001a. "Egypt: Country Assistance Strategy." Report No. 22163, World Bank, Washington, DC.

———. 2001b. "Egypt: Social and Structural Review." Report No. 22397, World Bank, Washington, DC.

———. 2000. "Socio-Economic Differences in Health, Nutrition, and Population in Egypt." HNP/Poverty Thematic Working Group Paper, World Bank, Washington, DC.

———. 1997a. "Arab Republic of Egypt: Country Economic Memorandum: Issues in Sustaining Growth." Report No. 16207-EGT, World Bank, Washington, DC.

———. 1997b. "Egypt: Country Assistance Strategy." Report No. 16533-EGT, World Bank, Washington, DC.

———. 1997c. "Egypt—Health Sector Reform Program." Report No. PID5893, World Bank, Washington, DC.

———. 1993. *World Development Report 1993: Investing in Health.* Washington, DC, and New York: World Bank and Oxford University Press.